THREE THEBAN PLAYS

Three Theban Plays

Sophocles

ANTIGONE

OEDIPUS THE KING

OEDIPUS AT COLONUS

Newly Translated by
Theodore Howard Banks

NEW YORK
OXFORD UNIVERSITY PRESS
1956

Library of Congress Catalogue Card Number: 56–7177

Eighth printing, 1965

Printed in the United States of America

To Merritt, Betsey, and David

PREFACE

THIS *book was written chiefly as a result of the support given me by my colleague Ralph D. Pendleton, Director of Dramatics. In the spring of 1949 I learned that he was planning to produce* ANTIGONE *the following year. I had long felt that there was no translation of Sophocles that was adequate both poetically and dramatically. The dialogue needed to be written in verse that preserved the idioms and cadence of spoken language; the choruses needed to be written as lyric poetry. As an experiment I went back to the long disused Greek which had been drilled into me as a schoolboy and wrote a version of one of the choruses. Mr. Pendleton's reception of this encouraged me to try my hand at the whole play. Indeed, he went so far as to start rehearsals before the translation was finished. Greater confidence hath no director than this. The production of* ANTIGONE *naturally led me on to the translation of the other two Theban plays.*

I am also greatly indebted to my colleagues Norman O. Brown, George N. Conklin, and John W. Spaeth for their help in problems of translation, and to my friends in general, who bore with me during the throes of composition. 'They could not choose but hear,' but at least they were very patient.

Finally, I am glad to record my thanks to the Trustees of Wesleyan University for a leave of absence during which a substantial part of this work was done.

THEODORE H. BANKS

Wesleyan University
Middletown, Connecticut
January 1956

CONTENTS

INTRODUCTION

GREEK DRAMA

GREEK civilization reached its peak in the Athens of the fifth century B.C., expressing itself in political organization, science, history, philosophy, and the arts: music, painting, sculpture, architecture, poetry, and drama. Some of the accomplishments of this period, tragedy for one, have never been surpassed. Yet since civilization is more than art, Greek tragedy cannot be fully understood without reference to other aspects of Athenian life.

Principally because the country was broken up by mountains, the Greeks never achieved national unity but remained divided into a large number of city-states, which were grouped into two systems of alliances headed by Athens and Sparta. These states consisted of a walled city that dominated a small, usually self-contained, country district. Attica, the district controlled by Athens, was exceptionally big, yet it was smaller than Rhode Island. The political situation was never stable, since there were constant minor hostilities and shifts of allegiance. Finally, the two major leagues clashed in the Peloponnesian War, which continued at intervals from 460 B.C. to 404 B.C. and ended in the destruction of Athens by Sparta. Although resting on a basis of slavery, these city-states, particularly Athens, attained a considerable degree of democracy. Many questions were decided directly by the vote of the whole body of the citizens, important political and religious offices were held in rotation, and a sense of belonging to a community was highly developed. Many things that we now think of as personal were then communal, and one of the most important of these was drama.

Plays were performed on two annual occasions, both religious, the more important of which was the spring festival lasting six days in honor of Dionysus, the god of wine and of the general fertility of nature. A large part of this festival was devoted to three poetical contests, presented in the theater of Dionysus. Seating seventeen thousand people, this was situated in a locality sacred to the god, an altar stood in the center of the orchestra, and the priest of Dionysus witnessed the performances from a seat in the front row. The three contests were in the dithyramb, an ode in honor of Dionysus, sung and danced by a chorus of fifty; in comedy; and in tragedy. On the last three days of the festival, three poets submitted four plays: three tragedies, either a trilogy or on independent themes, and a semi-comic piece called a satyr play. These plays were carefully rehearsed and elaborately produced, and were judged by a selected panel of citizens. To be chosen as one of the competing poets was in itself an honor; and to win first prize was a very high honor. The plays dealt with serious moral issues, illustrated by episodes in the lives of mythical heroes like Prometheus, or semi-historical members of ancient royal houses such as those of Athens, Thebes, or Mycenae. The main outlines of the stories were traditional and therefore familiar to the audience, but the poets were at liberty to modify or invent details. Given the circumstances of performance, the mood of the spectators must in general have been serious, although there were occasions on which they shouted down a play which did not come up to their expectations. Greek tragedy, then, was essentially civic and religious.

It was, however, far more than a succession of moral lessons. It was a highly developed art, though its form was severely limited and its conventions rigid. It was acted, as we have seen, in the open air, in a huge amphitheater. Necessarily, the actors would appear tiny, their expressions could not be seen, and their voices could hardly carry. Therefore, they wore shoes a foot high and masks in which were inserted small speaking trumpets. Presumably the acting was highly stylized, since the characters were almost symbolic, a quality emphasized by the masks. These characters were limited to eight or ten, exclusive of the chorus, and up to the time of Sophocles no more than two could appear or at any rate speak in any one scene. Indeed, the introduction of the third actor was one of Sophocles's chief contributions, since by this means he greatly increased the range of possible dramatic effects. The difference may be made clear by comparing his early *Antigone*, whose scenes are almost all dialogues, with the scenes in his late *Oedipus at Colonus* between Oedipus, Theseus, and Antigone, or between Oedipus, Polyneices, and Antigone. Yet the number of relationships that can be established between even three actors is still extremely limited. The plots were concerned with a single main episode in the life of the hero— for example, Oedipus's discovery of his identity—and the action usually, but not necessarily, took place in one day and in one place. Even with these conventions Greek drama is similar in its essentials to modern drama.

It is the chorus that marks off Greek drama as a distinct form of art. Just as modern drama originated in the singing in the medieval church services, so Greek drama originated in the singing of the dithyramb, which, as we have seen, was a religious ode. Gradually stanzas sung by separate sections of the chorus evolved into spoken dialogue, but even in the case of Aeschylus, Sophocles's immediate predecessor, the chorus, still numbering fifty, is so prominent that his plays are more like modern oratorios than dramas. Sophocles cut the chorus to fifteen and reduced its importance in the plot, but with him it remains an integral part of the play, since it consists of a group of people whose presence is dramatically appropriate. It is thought of as a unit and often speaks through the mouth of the chorus leader, or choragus. Occasionally it influences the action of the play through its advice, expostulation, and so forth, but its chief function is to react emotionally to the action taking place before it.

It philosophizes, expresses joy at the anticipated triumph of the hero or sorrow at his misfortune, prays to the gods, and the like. It expresses these emotions by singing or intoning intricate lyric poems to an accompaniment of music and dance steps. Except for a fragment of a Euripides chorus none of the music and no description of the dance patterns have survived, but we may reasonably assume that both music and dance had reached an artistic level comparable to the text. The suggestion has been made, for example, that Sophocles fixed the chorus at fifteen to allow a variety of unbalanced groupings. Obviously, such a combination of poetry, singing, music, and dancing must have had a powerful aesthetic effect. Even when the plays are merely read, the chorus serves not only to divide them into a series of contrasting and climactic scenes but also to introduce a great range of mood: triumphant, bitter, apprehensive, plaintive, etc. The effects are entirely different from those produced by the occasional songs in a Shakespearean play, since each Sophoclean ode occurs at a definite break in the action and serves as dramatic heightening as well as dramatic relief. It should be emphasized that the chorus is not the mouthpiece of Sophocles, expressing his personal feelings, but a dramatic entity, expressing emotions natural under the circumstances in which it finds itself. Everything considered, the closest modern equivalent to a tragedy of Sophocles is not a play but a grand opera.

THE LIFE OF SOPHOCLES (c. 496-406 B.C.)

Although Sophocles lived to the extreme age of ninety, and although he was a prominent figure in the life of his time, we know very little about him. He was noted for his youthful beauty and his skill in dancing and music. He led, with his lyre, the paean celebrating the naval victory over the Persians at Salamis. He took part, as was customary, in the acting of his plays but was forced to stop because of his weak voice. As a citizen he held the usual offices, being General at least twice. He was associated in some way with the cult of Asclepius, the god of healing. These facts, together with some rather trivial anecdotes, are all that we know about his private life.

His artistic career was extraordinarily prolific and successful, although only seven of one hundred and twenty-odd plays have survived. In the annual competition during the festival of Dionysus, he won first place twenty times (and we must remember that each victory involved four of his plays), and was never worse than second. The three plays in this volume were written over a period of nearly forty years: *Antigone* about 441 B.C., *Oedipus the King* about 430 B.C., and *Oedipus at Colonus* about 409 B.C., when Sophocles was more than eighty years of age. Not only is this order of composition not the chronological order of events, but the plays are independent artistic wholes, whose details cannot be reconciled, for example, the relative ages of Creon, Oedipus, and his children; or the character of Creon. It is for these reasons that the plays are here printed in the order of their composition.

THE ROYAL FAMILY OF THEBES

About the House of Thebes an extensive cycle of legends developed. The first King was the mythical hero Cadmus. In searching for his sister Europa, whom Zeus had abducted, he came to the site of Thebes, where an oracle of Delphi instructed him to establish a city. While performing the sacrificial ceremonies, he killed a serpent sacred to Ares and, directed by Athene, sowed its teeth. Immediately a crowd of armed men sprang up, who fought among themselves until only five remained alive. These survivors, together with Cadmus, became the ancestors of the Thebans. To atone for killing the serpent Cadmus had to serve Ares for eight years, at the end of which time he married Harmonia, daughter of Ares and Aphrodite. Further myths, some of which involved sin and punishment by the gods, told of the later life of Cadmus and Harmonia and of their numerous children.

OEDIPUS

One grandson of Cadmus was Labdacus, whose son was Laius, the father of Oedipus. Oedipus was perhaps the most famous of all the figures of Greek legend. The earliest reference to an integral story about him is found in the Odyssey (11.271ff.). This story was fully developed in a series of later epics, which have not survived, and in dramas. Aeschylus wrote a trilogy consisting of the *Laius*, the *Oedipus* (both lost), and the extant *Seven against Thebes*. The plays of Euripides on the subject are also lost, as are at least eight or nine tragedies entitled *Oedipus* by other poets.

Laius, while visiting Pelops, a grandson of Zeus, abducted Chrysippus, the son of Pelops. Because of this crime, Laius was informed by the oracle of Delphi that he would be killed by his own son. To avoid this fate he had Oedipus, as soon as he was born, maimed by pinning his feet together with a peg (Oedipus means swollen foot) and left to die in the wilds of Mount Cithaeron. Oedipus, however, was rescued and brought up in Corinth, believing himself to be the son of King Polybus. When he heard from the oracle that he was to kill his father and marry his mother, he fled from Corinth. On his way to Thebes he met King Laius and killed him in a roadside quarrel. He next encountered the Sphinx, a monster half-woman half-lion, who killed every passer-by unable to answer her riddle. By giving the correct answer Oedipus caused the Sphinx to commit suicide and thus freed Thebes from her scourge. For this service he was made King of Thebes and was married to Jocasta, the widow of King Laius, his mother. They had two sons, Polyneices and Eteocles, and two daughters, Antigone and Ismene. When their incestuous relationship was discovered, Jocasta hanged herself and Oedipus stabbed out his eyes. The second of the plays in this volume, *Oedipus the King*, is concerned with this discovery. In the next generation the curse continued to operate.

After the death or banishment of Oedipus (the versions differ), Creon, the brother of Jocasta, became regent during the minorities of Polyneices and Eteocles. Creon was himself of the royal family, since he and Jocasta were cousins of Laius. When the boys came of age, they fought for their father's kingship. Eteocles drove out Polyneices, who went to Argos, where he raised an army against Thebes. The third play, *Oedipus at Colonus*, is concerned with the death of Oedipus just before the final battle at the city gates. The invaders were defeated, the two brothers killing each other. The first play, *Antigone*, opens on the morning after this battle and deals with the death of Antigone. Ultimately Thebes was destroyed by the sons of the leaders of the first hostile army.

One important fact about the Oedipus legend should be stressed. It is very unlikely that Sophocles felt that Oedipus was fated to kill his father and marry his mother. The word 'fate' occurs often in the plays in this volume, but it was used as loosely in Sophocles's time as it is now. It is true that the gods often intervened directly in human affairs so that their arbitrary will determined a man's lot in life. At the same time, there existed an impersonal fate, upholding moral order in the universe, before which even the gods were powerless. In general, it is probably best to think of the gods, or their prophets like Tiresias, as foretelling what was going to happen in the future but not as compelling it to happen. A similar situation exists today. All Christians believe in the omniscience of God, which must include his knowledge of the future, but few will admit that God's foreknowledge limits man's free will. To maintain that Oedipus could not possibly avoid his fate, once it had been announced by the oracle, is to destroy his tragic dignity. If he had been merely a helpless pawn, he could hardly have fitted Aristotle's definition of a tragic hero: 'A man who is highly renowned and prosperous, but one who is not pre-eminently virtuous and just, whose misfortune, however, is brought upon him not by vice and depravity but by some error of judgment or frailty.' Oedipus commits an error of judgment in marrying anyone at all, considering what the oracle had said, and he has the frailty (the tragic flaw) of a quick temper, but these faults are not serious enough to warrant the horrors he has to endure. Laius may possibly be justly punished, but so far as Oedipus is concerned the problem of innocent suffering remains unsolved. In this connection it is interesting to notice that in *Oedipus at Colonus* Oedipus insists that he has always been innocent, though he is as hot-tempered as ever. In *Antigone* the problem does not arise. Tiresias prophesies truly that Creon will pay for his sacrilege by the death of his son, and the Chorus speaks of the gods as striking down a whole race and sending suffering upon the house of Oedipus, a fate that does not loosen its hold through generations, and yet it would never occur to a spectator, and does not seem to have occurred to a critic, that either Creon or Antigone lacks free will. The reasonable conclusion, therefore, seems to be that Sophocles, like almost all of us, believed that a human being was a responsible moral agent, neither insignificant nor helpless, but on the contrary dignified and even noble.

THE TRANSLATION

Since translation is an art, the translator must write primarily to satisfy himself, and the particular form he chooses cannot be logically defended. It can only be described. The form of these translations is as follows: most of the dialogue is in blank verse, and special care was taken to catch the idioms and cadences of spoken, rather than written, language. Some dialogue, in the passages where there is a change of meter in the original, is in heroic couplet, heroic quatrains, or irregular rhymed stanzas.

The choruses and a number of lyric passages in the dialogue are in rhymed stanzas. These stanzas are in pairs and thus preserve a distinctive feature of the Greek. The first stanza, the strophe, sets the rhythmic pattern, and the second stanza, the antistrophe, repeats it exactly. The pattern of stanzas three and four is likewise identical but differs from the first pattern. Occasionally a chorus has an odd stanza, an epode, with an individual pattern. There is, then, repetition within each chorus, but the rhyme scheme and rhythms of one chorus are never repeated in any other. Each chorus is a lyric poem which differs in mood, and therefore in form, from all the rest.

The choruses are distinguished from the dialogue in two other ways. Because they are lyric poems, in which people are not so much speaking as singing, their vocabulary is somewhat fuller and more elaborate. Also, in them, the translation is of necessity less close, since the thought must be paraphrased or expanded to provide rhymes. Rhymed stanzas contrast sharply with the dialogue, however, and this contrast provides an aesthetic effect comparable to that of the Greek. Furthermore, experience with this text has shown that when the plays are produced the choruses lend themselves readily to group speaking, to musical accompaniment, and to dance interpretation. The resulting aesthetic effect is markedly unlike that produced by a modern play. To sum up, therefore, it may be well to repeat what was said earlier. Even with all the suspense, the clash of personalities, and the climactic emotion of Greek drama, the contemporary art form that most closely resembles it is grand opera.

Antigone

CHARACTERS IN THE PLAY

CREON, *King of Thebes, brother of* JOCASTA, *the mother and wife of* OEDIPUS

EURYDICE, *Queen of Thebes, wife of* CREON

HAEMON, *son of* CREON

ANTIGONE
ISMENE
} *daughters of* OEDIPUS *and* JOCASTA

TIRESIAS, *a prophet*

BOY, *attendant of* TIRESIAS

GUARD

MESSENGER

CHORUS *of Theban Elders*

ATTENDANTS

ANTIGONE

SCENE: *Courtyard of the royal palace at Thebes. Daybreak.*

Enter ANTIGONE *and* ISMENE

ANTIGONE:

    Dear sister! Dear Ismene! How many evils
    Our father, Oedipus, bequeathed to us!
    And is there one of them—do you know of one
    That Zeus has not showered down upon our heads?
    I have seen pain, dishonor, shame, and ruin,
    I have seen them all, in what we have endured.
    And now comes this new edict by the King
    Proclaimed throughout the city. Have you heard?
    Do you not know, even yet, our friends are threatened?
    They are to meet the fate of enemies.   10

ISMENE:

    Our friends, Antigone? No, I have heard
    Nothing about them either good or bad.
    I have no news except that we two sisters
    Lost our two brothers when they killed each other.
    I know the Argive army fled last night,
    But what that means, or whether it makes my life
    Harder or easier, I cannot tell.

ANTIGONE:

    This I was sure of. So I brought you here
    Beyond the palace gates to talk alone.

ISMENE:

    What is the matter? I know you are deeply troubled.   20

ANTIGONE:

    Yes, for our brothers' fate. Creon has given
    An honored burial to one, to the other
    Only unburied shame. Eteocles
    Is laid in the earth with all the rites observed
    That give him his due honor with the dead.
    But the decree concerning Polyneices
    Published through Thebes is that his wretched body
    Shall lie unmourned, unwept, unsepulchered.
    Sweet will he seem to the vultures when they find him,
    A welcome feast that they are eager for.   30
    This is the edict the good Creon uttered
    For your observance and for mine—yes, mine.
    He is coming here himself to make it plain
    To those who have not heard. Nor does he think it

Of little consequence, because whoever
Does not obey is doomed to death by stoning.
Now you can show you are worthy of your birth,
Or bring disgrace upon a noble house.

ISMENE:

What can I do, Antigone? As things are,
What can I do that would be of any help?   40

ANTIGONE:

You can decide if you will share my task.

ISMENE:

What do you mean? What are you planning to do?

ANTIGONE:

I intend to give him burial. Will you help?

ISMENE:

To give him burial! Against the law?

ANTIGONE:

He is our brother. I will do my duty,
Yours too, perhaps. I never will be false.

ISMENE:

Creon forbids it! You are too rash, too headstrong.

ANTIGONE:

He has no right to keep me from my own.

ISMENE:

Antigone! Think! Think how our father perished
In scorn and hatred when his sins, that he   50
Himself discovered, drove him to strike blind
His eyes by his own hand. Think how his mother,
His wife—both names were hers—ended her life
Shamefully hanging in a twisted noose.
Think of that dreadful day when our two brothers,
Our wretched brothers, fought and fell together,
Each slayer and each slain. And now we too,
Left all alone, think how in turn we perish,
If, in defiance of the law, we brave
The power of the commandment of a king.   60
O think Antigone! We who are women
Should not contend with men; we who are weak
Are ruled by the stronger, so that we must obey
In this and in matters that are yet more bitter.
And so I pray the dead to pardon me
If I obey our rulers, since I must.
To be too bold in what we do is madness.

ANTIGONE:

I will not urge you. And I would not thank you
For any help that you might care to give me.
Do what you please, but I will bury him,   70

And if I die for that, I shall be happy.
Loved, I shall rest beside the one I loved.
My crime is innocence, for I owe the dead
Longer allegiance than I owe the living.
With the dead I lie forever. Live, if you choose,
Dishonoring the laws the gods have hallowed.

ISMENE:

No, I dishonor nothing. But to challenge
Authority—I have not strength enough.

ANTIGONE:

Then make that your excuse. I will go heap
The earth above the brother that I love.   80

ISMENE:

O Sister, Sister! How I fear for you!

ANTIGONE:

No, not for me. Set your own life in order.

ISMENE:

Well then, at least, tell no one of your plan.
Keep it close hidden, as I too will keep it.

ANTIGONE:

Oh! Publish it! Proclaim it to the world!
Then I will hate you less than for your silence.

ISMENE:

Your heart is hot for deeds that chill the blood.

ANTIGONE:

I know that I give pleasure where I should.

ISMENE:

Yes, if you can, but you will try in vain.

ANTIGONE:

When my strength fails, then I shall try no longer.   90

ISMENE:

A hopeless task should never be attempted.

ANTIGONE:

Your words have won their just reward: my hatred
And the long-lasting hatred of the dead.
But leave me and the folly that is mine
To undergo the worst that can befall me.
I shall not suffer an ignoble death.

ISMENE:

Go then, Antigone, if you must go.
And yet remember, though your act is foolish,
That those who love you do so with all their hearts.

Exeunt ANTIGONE *and* ISMENE. *Enter* CHORUS

CHORUS:

Sunbeam, eye of the golden day, on Thebes the seven-gated,   100
　On Dircé's streams you have dawned at last, O fairest of light.

Dawned on our foes, who had come enflamed by the quarrel of
   Polyneices,
 Shone on their glittering arms, made swifter their headlong flight.
  From Argos they came with their white shields flashing,
   Their helmets, crested with horsehair, agleam:
  An army that flew like a snow-white eagle
   Across our borders with shrilling scream.

Above our roofs it soared, at our gates with greedy jaws it was gaping;
 But before their spears tasted our blood, and before our circle of
   towers
Felt the flame of their torches, they turned to flight. The foes of the
   Theban dragon   110
 Found the surge and clamor of battle too fierce for their feebler
   powers.
  For Zeus, who abhors a proud tongue's boasting,
   Seeing their river of armor flow
  Clashing and golden, struck with his lightning
   To silence the shout of our foremost foe.

He crashed to the earth with his torch, who had scaled the top of our
   ramparts,
 Raging in frenzy against us, breathing tempestuous hate,
Raging and threatening in vain. And mighty Ares, our ally,
 Dealing havoc around him, apportioned to other foemen their fate.
  For at seven portals, their seven leaders,   120
   Down to the earth their bronze arms threw
  In tribute to Zeus, the lord of the battle;
   Save the fated brothers, the wretched two,
  Who went to their common doom together,
   Each wielding a spear that the other slew.

Now glorious Victory smiles upon jubilant Thebes rich in chariots.
 Let us give free rein to our joy, forgetting our late-felt war;
Let us visit in night-long chorus the temples of all the immortals,
 With Bacchus, who shakes the land in the dances, going before.
  But behold! The son of Monoeceus approaches,   130
   Creon, the new-crowned King of the land,
  Made King by new fortunes the gods have allotted.
   What step has he pondered? What has he planned
  To lay before us, his council of elders,
   Who have gathered together at his command?

           Enter CREON

CREON:
   Elders of Thebes, our city has been tossed

6

By a tempestuous ocean, but the gods
Have steadied it once more and made it safe.
You, out of all the citizens, I have summoned,
Because I knew that you once reverenced   140
The sovereignty of Laius, and that later,
When Oedipus was King and when he perished,
Your steadfast loyalty upheld his children.
And now his sons have fallen, each one stained
By his brother's blood, killed by his brother's hand,
So that the sovereignty devolves on me,
Since I by birth am nearest to the dead.
Certainly no man can be fully known,
Known in his soul, his will, his intellect,
Until he is tested and has proved himself   150
In statesmanship. Because a city's ruler,
Instead of following the wisest counsel,
May through some fear keep silent. Such a man
I think contemptible. And one whose friend
Has stronger claims upon him than his country,
Him I consider worthless. As for me,
I swear by Zeus, forever all-beholding,
That I would not keep silence, if I saw
Ruin instead of safety drawing near us;
Nor would I think an enemy of the state   160
Could be my friend. For I remember this:
Our country bears us all securely onward,
And only while it sails a steady course
Is friendship possible. Such are the laws
By which I guard the greatness of the city.
And kindred to them is the proclamation
That I have made to all the citizens
Concerning the two sons of Oedipus:
Eteocles, who has fallen in our defence,
Bravest of warriors, shall be entombed   170
With every honor, every offering given
That may accompany the noble dead
Down to their rest. But as for Polyneices,
He came from exile eager to consume
The city of his fathers with his fire
And all the temples of his fathers' gods,
Eager to drink deep of his kindred's blood,
Eager to drag us off to slavery.
To this man, therefore, nothing shall be given.
None shall lament him, none shall do him honor.   180
He shall be left without a grave, his corpse
Devoured by birds and dogs, a loathsome sight.

Such is my will. For never shall the wicked
Be given more approval than the just,
If I have power to stop it. But whoever
Feels in his heart affection for his city
Shall be rewarded both in life and death.

CHORUS:

Creon, son of Menoeceus, it has pleased you
So to pass judgment on our friend and foe.
And you may give commands to all of us,   190
The living and the dead. Your will is law.

CREON:

Then see that this command is carried out.

CHORUS:

Sir, lay that burden on some younger man.

CREON:

Sentries have been assigned to guard the body.

CHORUS:

Then what additional duty would you give us?

CREON:

Never to countenance the disobedient.

CHORUS:

Who is so stupid as to long for death?

CREON:

Death is indeed the punishment. Yet men
Have often been destroyed by hope of gain.

Enter GUARD

GUARD:

My Lord, I cannot say that I have hurried,   200
Or that my running has made me lose my breath.
I often stopped to think, and turned to go back.
I stood there talking to myself: 'You fool,'
I said, 'Why do you go to certain death?'
And then: 'You idiot, are you still delaying?
If someone else tells Creon, you will suffer.'
I changed my mind this way, getting here slowly,
Making a short road long. But still, at last,
I did decide to come. And though my story
Is nothing much to tell, yet I will tell it.   210
One thing I know. I must endure my fate,
But nothing more than that can happen to me.

CREON:

What is the matter? What is troubling you?

GUARD:

Please let me tell you first about myself.

I did not do it. I did not see who did.
It is not right for me to be punished for it.

CREON:

You take good care not to expose yourself.
Your news must certainly be something strange.

GUARD:

Yes, it is strange—dreadful. I cannot speak.

CREON:

Oh, tell it, will you? Tell it and go away!   220

GUARD:

Well, it is this. Someone has buried the body,
Just now, and gone—has sprinkled it with dust
And given it other honors it should have.

CREON:

What are you saying? Who has dared to do it?

GUARD:

I cannot tell. Nothing was to be seen:
No mark of pickaxe, no spot where a spade
Had turned the earth. The ground was hard and dry,
Unbroken—not a trace of any wheels—
No sign to show who did it. When the sentry
On the first watch discovered it and told us,   230
We were struck dumb with fright. For he was hidden
Not by a tomb but a light coat of dust,
As if a pious hand had scattered it.
There were no tracks of any animal,
A dog or wild beast that had come to tear him.
We all began to quarrel, and since no one
Was there to stop us, nearly came to blows.
Everyone was accused, and everyone
Denied his guilt. We could discover nothing.
We were quite willing to handle red-hot iron,   240
To walk through fire, to swear by all the gods
That we were innocent of the deed itself,
And innocent of taking any part
In planning it or doing it. At last
One of us spoke. We trembled and hung our heads,
For he was right; we could not argue with him,
Yet his advice was bound to cause us trouble.
He told us all this had to be reported,
Not kept a secret. We all agreed to that.
We drew lots for it, and I had no luck.   250
I won the prize and was condemned to come.
So here I stand, unwilling, because I know
The bringer of bad news is never welcome.

CHORUS:

Sir, as he spoke, I have been wondering.
Can this be, possibly, the work of gods?

CREON:

Be silent! Before you madden me! You are old.
Would you be senseless also? What you say
Is unendurable. You say the gods
Cared for this corpse. Then was it for reward,
Mighty to match his mighty services,   260
That the gods covered him? He who came to burn
Their pillared temples and their votive offerings,
Ravage their land, and trample down the state.
Or is it your opinion that the gods
Honor the wicked? Inconceivable!
However, from the first, some citizens
Who found it difficult to endure this edict,
Muttered against me, shaking their heads in secret,
Instead of bowing down beneath the yoke,
Obedient and contented with my rule.   270
These are the men who are responsible,
For I am certain they have bribed the guards
To bury him. Nothing is worse than money.
Money lays waste to cities, banishes
Men from their homes, indoctrinates the heart,
Perverting honesty to works of shame,
Showing men how to practice villainy,
Subduing them to every godless deed.
But all those men who got their pay for this
Need have no doubt their turn to pay will come.   280
(to the GUARD) Now, you. As I still honor Zeus the King,
I tell you, and I swear it solemnly,
Either you find the man who did this thing,
The very man, and bring him here to me,
Or you will not just die. Before you die,
You will be tortured until you have explained
This outrage; so that later when you steal
You will know better where to look for money
And not expect to find it everywhere.
Ill-gotten wealth brings ruin and not safety.   290

GUARD:

Sir, may I speak? Or shall I merely go?

CREON:

You can say nothing that is not offensive.

GUARD:

Do I offend your hearing or your heart?

CREON:

Is it your business to define the spot?

GUARD:

The criminal hurts your heart, and I your ears.

CREON:

Still talking? Why, you must have been born talking!

GUARD:

Perhaps. But I am not the guilty man.

CREON:

You are. And what is more you sold yourself.

GUARD:

You have judged me, sir, and have misjudged me, too.

CREON:

Be clever about judging if you care to.   300
But you will say that treachery leads to sorrow
Unless you find the man and show him to me.

Exit CREON

GUARD:

Finding him is the best thing that could happen.
Fate will decide. But however that may be,
You never are going to see me here again.
I have escaped! I could not have hoped for that.
I owe the gods my thanks for guarding me.

Exit GUARD

CHORUS:

Many the marvelous things; but none that can be
  More of a marvel than man! This being that braves
With the south wind of winter the whitened streaks of the sea,   310
  Threading his way through the troughs of engulfing waves.
And the earth most ancient, the eldest of all the gods,
  Earth, undecaying, unwearied, he wears away with his toil;
Forward and back with his plowshare, year after year, he plods,
  With his horses turning the soil.

Man in devising excels. The birds of the air,
  That light-minded race, he entangles fast in his toils.
Wild creatures he catches, casting about them his snare,
  And the salt-sea brood he nets in his woven coils.
The tireless bull he has tamed, and the beast whose lair   320
  Is hidden deep in the wilds, who roams in the wooded hills.
He has fitted a yoke that the neck of the shaggy-maned horse
      will bear;
  He is master of all through his skills.

He has taught himself speech, and wind-like thought, and the lore
  Of ruling a town. He has fled the arrows of rain,
The searching arrows of frost he need fear no more,
  That under a starry sky are endured with pain.

11

Provision for all he has made—unprovided for naught,
　　Save death itself, that in days to come will take shape.
From obscure and deep-seated disease he has subtly wrought　　330
　　A way of escape.

Resourceful and skilled, with an inconceivable art,
　　He follows his course to a good or an evil end.
When he holds the canons of justice high in his heart
　　And has sworn to the gods the laws of the land to defend,
Proud stands his city; without a city is he
　　Who with ugliness, rashness, or evil dishonors the day.
Let me shun his thoughts. Let him share no hearthstone with me,
　　Who acts in this way!

CHORUS:

　　Look there! Look there! What portent can this be?　　340
　　Antigone! I know her, it is she!
　　Daughter of Oedipus a prisoner brought?
　　You defied Creon? You in folly caught?

Enter GUARD *with* ANTIGONE

GUARD:

　　　　She did it. Here she is. We caught this girl
　　　　As she was burying him. Where is the King?

CHORUS:

　　　　Leaving the palace there, just as we need him.

Enter CREON

CREON:

　　　　Why do you need my presence? What has happened?

GUARD:

　　　　My Lord, no one should take a solemn oath
　　　　Not to do something, for his second thoughts
　　　　Make him a liar. I vowed not to hurry back.　　350
　　　　I had been battered by your storm of threats.
　　　　But when a joy comes that exceeds our hopes,
　　　　No other happiness can equal it.
　　　　So I have broken my vow. I have returned,
　　　　Bringing this girl along. She was discovered
　　　　Busy with all the rites of burial.
　　　　There was no casting lots, no, not this time!
　　　　Such luck as this was mine and no one else's.
　　　　Now sir, take her yourself, examine her,
　　　　Convict her, do what you like. But as for me,　　360
　　　　I have the right to a complete acquittal.

12

CREON:

    This is the girl you caught? How? Where was she?

GUARD:

    Burying the dead man, just as I have told you.

CREON:

    Do you mean that? Or have you lost your mind?

GUARD:

    Your order was that he should not be buried.
    I saw her bury him. Is that all clear?

CREON:

    How was she seen? You caught her in the act?

GUARD:

    This was what happened. When we had gotten back,
    With your threats following us, we swept away
    The dust that covered him. We left him bare,   370
    A rotting corpse. And then we sat to windward,
    Up on the hillside, to avoid the stench.
    All of us were alert, and kept awake
    Threatening each other. No one could get careless.
    So the time passed, until the blazing sun
    Stood at the zenith, and the heat was burning.
    Then suddenly the wind came in a blast,
    Lifting a cloud of dust up from the earth,
    Troubling the sky and choking the whole plain,
    Stripping off all the foliage of the woods,   380
    Filling the breadth of heaven. We closed our eyes
    And bore the affliction that the gods had sent us.
    When it had finally stopped, we saw this girl.
    She wailed aloud with a sharp, bitter cry,
    The cry a bird gives seeing its empty nest
    Robbed of its brood. And she too, when she saw
    The naked body, was loud in her lament
    And cursed the men who had uncovered him.
    Quickly she sprinkled him with dust, and then
    Lifting a pitcher, poured out three libations   390
    To do him honor. When we ran and caught her,
    She was unterrified. When we accused her
    Both of her earlier and her present act,
    She made no effort to deny the charges.
    I am part glad, part sorry. It is good
    To find that you yourself have gotten clear,
    But to bring trouble on your friends is hard.
    However, nothing counts except my safety.

CREON (*to* ANTIGONE):

    You there. You, looking at the ground. Tell me.
    Do you admit this or deny it? Which?   400

ANTIGONE:

Yes, I admit it. I do not deny it.

CREON (*to* GUARD):

Go. You are free. The charge is dropped.

Exit GUARD

Now you,

Answer this question. Make your answer brief.
You knew there was a law forbidding this?

ANTIGONE:

Of course I knew it. Why not? It was public.

CREON:

And you have dared to disobey the law?

ANTIGONE:

Yes. For this law was not proclaimed by Zeus,
Or by the gods who rule the world below.
I do not think your edicts have such power
That they can override the laws of heaven,   410
Unwritten and unfailing, laws whose life
Belongs not to today or yesterday
But to time everlasting; and no man
Knows the first moment that they had their being.
If I transgressed these laws because I feared
The arrogance of man, how to the gods
Could I make satisfaction? Well I know,
Being a mortal, that I have to die,
Even without your proclamations. Yet
If I must die before my time is come,   420
That is a blessing. Because to one who lives,
As I live, in the midst of sorrows, death
Is of necessity desirable.
For me, to face death is a trifling pain
That does not trouble me. But to have left
The body of my brother, my own brother,
Lying unburied would be bitter grief.
And if these acts of mine seem foolish to you,
Perhaps a fool accuses me of folly.

CHORUS:

The violent daughter of a violent father,   430
She cannot bend before a storm of evils.

CREON (*to* ANTIGONE):

Stubborn? Self-willed? People like that, I tell you,
Are the first to come to grief. The hardest iron,
Baked in the fire, most quickly flies to pieces.
An unruly horse is taught obedience
By a touch of the curb. How can you be so proud?

You, a mere slave? (*to* CHORUS) She was well schooled already
In insolence, when she defied the law.
And now look at her! Boasting, insolent,
Exulting in what she did. And if she triumphs
And goes unpunished, I am no man—she is.   440
If she were more than niece, if she were closer
Than anyone who worships at my altar,
She would not even then escape her doom,
A dreadful death. Nor would her sister. Yes,
Her sister had a share in burying him.
(*to* ATTENDANT) Go bring her here. I have just seen her, raving,
Beside herself. Even before they act,
Traitors who plot their treason in the dark
Betray themselves like that. Detestable!
(*to* ANTIGONE) But hateful also is an evil-doer   450
Who, caught red-handed, glorifies the crime.

ANTIGONE:
    Now you have caught me, will you do more than kill me?
CREON:
    No, only that. With that I am satisfied.
ANTIGONE:
    Then why do you delay? You have said nothing
    I do not hate. I pray you never will.
    And you hate what I say. Yet how could I
    Have won more splendid honor than by giving
    Due burial to my brother? All men here
    Would grant me their approval, if their lips
    Were not sealed up in fear. But you, a king,   460
    Blessed by good fortune in much else besides,
    Can speak and act with perfect liberty.
CREON:
    All of these Thebans disagree with you.
ANTIGONE:
    No. They agree, but they control their tongues.
CREON:
    You feel no shame in acting without their help?
ANTIGONE:
    I feel no shame in honoring a brother.
CREON:
    Another brother died who fought against him.
ANTIGONE:
    Two brothers. The two sons of the same parents.
CREON:
    Honor to one is outrage to the other.
ANTIGONE:
    Eteocles will not feel himself dishonored.   470

CREON:

What! When his rites are offered to a traitor?

ANTIGONE:

It was his brother, not his slave, who died.

CREON:

One who attacked the land that he defended.

ANTIGONE:

The gods still wish those rites to be performed.

CREON:

Are the just pleased with the unjust as their equals?

ANTIGONE:

That may be virtuous in the world below.

CREON:

No. Even there a foe is never a friend.

ANTIGONE:

I am not made for hatred but for love.

CREON:

Then go down to the dead. If you must love,
Love them. While I yet live, no woman rules me.   480

CHORUS:

Look there. Ismene, weeping as sisters weep.
The shadow of a cloud of grief lies deep
On her face, darkly flushed; and in her pain
Her tears are falling like a flood of rain.

Enter ISMENE *and* ATTENDANTS

CREON:

You viper! Lying hidden in my house,
Sucking my blood in secret, while I reared,
Unknowingly, two subverters of my throne.
Do you confess that you have taken part
In this man's burial, or deny it? Speak.

ISMENE:

If she will recognize my right to say so,   490
I shared the action and I share the blame.

ANTIGONE:

No. That would not be just. I never let you
Take any part in what you disapproved of.

ISMENE:

In your calamity, I am not ashamed
To stand beside you, beaten by this tempest.

ANTIGONE:

The dead are witnesses of what I did,
To love in words alone is not enough.

ISMENE:

Do not reject me, Sister! Let me die
Beside you, and do honor to the dead.

ANTIGONE:

No. You will neither share my death nor claim   500
What I have done. My death will be sufficient.

ISMENE:

What happiness can I have when you are gone?

ANTIGONE:

Ask Creon that. He is the one you value.

ISMENE:

Do you gain anything by taunting me?

ANTIGONE:

Ah, no! By taunting you, I hurt myself.

ISMENE:

How can I help you? Tell me what I can do.

ANTIGONE:

Protect yourself. I do not grudge your safety.

ISMENE:

Antigone! Shall I not share your fate?

ANTIGONE:

We both have made our choices: life, and death.

ISMENE:

At least I tried to stop you. I protested.   510

ANTIGONE:

Some have approved your way; and others, mine.

ISMENE:

Yet now I share your guilt. I too am ruined.

ANTIGONE:

Take courage. Live your life. But I long since
Gave myself up to death to help the dead.

CREON:

One of them has just lost her senses now.
The other has been foolish all her life.

ISMENE:

We cannot always use our reason clearly.
Suffering confuses us and clouds our minds.

CREON:

It clouds your mind. You join in her wrong-doing.

ISMENE:

How is life possible without my sister?   520

CREON:

Your sister? You have no sister. She is dead.

ISMENE:

Then you will kill the wife your son has chosen?

CREON:

Yes. There are other fields that he can plow.

ISMENE:

He will not find such an enduring love.

CREON:
> A wicked woman for my son? No, never!

ANTIGONE:
> O Haemon, Haemon! How your father wrongs you!

CREON:
> You and your marriage! Let me hear no more!

CHORUS:
> You are unyielding? You will take her from him?

CREON:
> Death will act for me. Death will stop the marriage.

CHORUS:
> It seems, then, you have sentenced her to death.   530

CREON:
> Yes. And my sentence you yourselves accepted.
> Take them inside. From now on, they are women,
> And have no liberty. For even the bold
> Seek an escape when they see death approaching.

> *Exeunt* ANTIGONE, ISMENE, *and* ATTENDANTS

CHORUS:
> Blesséd the life that has no evil known,
> For the gods, striking, strike down a whole race—
> Doomed parent and doomed child both overthrown.
> As when the fierce breath of the winds of Thrace
> Across the darkness of the sea has blown
> A rushing surge; black sand from deep below   540
> Comes boiling up; wind-beaten headlands moan,
> Fronting the full shock of the billow's blow.

> The race of Oedipus, from days of old,
> To long dead sorrows add new sorrows' weight.
> Some god has sent them sufferings manifold.
> None may release another, for their fate
> Through generations loosens not its hold.
> Now is their last root cut, their last light fled,
> Because of frenzy's curse, words overbold,
> And dust, the gods' due, on the bloodstained dead.   550

> O Zeus, what human sin restricts thy might?
> Thou art unsnared by all-ensnaring sleep
> Or tireless months. Unaging thou dost keep
> Thy court in splendor of Olympian light.
> And as this law was true when time began,
> Tomorrow and forever it shall be:
> Naught beyond measure in the life of man
> From fate goes free.

For hope, wide-ranging, that brings good to some,
To many is a false lure of desire   560
　　Light-minded, giddy; and until the fire
Scorches their feet, they know not what will come.
　　Wise is the famous adage: that to one
Whom the gods madden, evil, soon or late,
　　Seems good; then can he but a moment shun
　　　　The stroke of fate.

　　But Haemon comes, of your two sons the last.
Is his heart heavy for the sentence passed
　　Upon Antigone, his promised bride,
And for his hope of marriage now denied?   570

Enter HAEMON

CREON:

We soon shall know better than seers could tell us.
My son, Antigone is condemned to death.
Nothing can change my sentence. Have you learned
Her fate and come here in a storm of anger,
Or do you love me and support my acts?

HAEMON:

Father, I am your son. Your greater knowledge
Will trace the pathway that I mean to follow.
My marriage cannot be of more importance
Than to be guided always by your wisdom.

CREON:

Yes, Haemon, this should be the law you live by!   580
In all things to obey your father's will.
Men pray for children round them in their homes
Only to see them dutiful and quick
With hatred to requite their father's foe,
With honor to repay their father's friend.
But what is there to say of one whose children
Prove to be valueless? That he has fathered
Grief for himself and laughter for his foes.
Then, Haemon, do not, at the lure of pleasure,
Unseat your reason for a woman's sake.   590
This comfort soon grows cold in your embrace:
A wicked wife to share your bed and home.
Is there a deeper wound than to find worthless
The one you love? Turn from this girl with loathing,
As from an enemy, and let her go
To get a husband in the world below.
For I have found her openly rebellious,
Her only out of all the city. Therefore,

I will not break the oath that I have sworn.
I will have her killed. Vainly she will invoke   600
The bond of kindred blood the gods make sacred.
If I permit disloyalty to breed
In my own house, I nurture it in strangers.
He who is righteous with his kin is righteous
In the state also. Therefore, I cannot pardon
One who does violence to the laws or thinks
To dictate to his rulers; for whoever
May be the man appointed by the city,
That man must be obeyed in everything,
Little or great, just or unjust. And surely   610
He who was thus obedient would be found
As good a ruler as he was a subject;
And in a storm of spears he would stand fast
With loyal courage at his comrade's side.
But disobedience is the worst of evils.
For it is this that ruins cities; this
Makes our homes desolate; armies of allies
Through this break up in rout. But most men find
Their happiness and safety in obedience.
Therefore we must support the law, and never   620
Be beaten by a woman. It is better
To fall by a man's hand, if we must fall,
Than to be known as weaker than a girl.

CHORUS:

We may in our old age have lost our judgment,
And yet to us you seem to have spoken wisely.

HAEMON:

The gods have given men the gift of reason,
Greatest of all things that we call our own.
I have no skill, nor do I wish to have it,
To show where you have spoken wrongly. Yet
Some other's thought, beside your own, might prove   630
To be of value. Therefore it is my duty,
My natural duty as your son, to notice,
On your behalf, all that men say, or do,
Or find to blame. For your frown frightens them,
So that the citizen dares not say a word
That would offend you. I can hear, however,
Murmurs in darkness and laments for her.
They say: 'No woman ever less deserved
Her doom, no woman ever was to die
So shamefully for deeds so glorious.   640
For when her brother fell in bloody battle,
She would not let his body lie unburied

To be devoured by carrion dogs or birds.
Does such a woman not deserve reward,
Reward of golden honor?' This I hear,
A rumor spread in secrecy and darkness.
Father, I prize nothing in life so highly
As your well-being. How can children have
A nobler honor than their father's fame
Or father than his son's? Then do not think   650
Your mood must never alter; do not feel
Your word, and yours alone, must be correct.
For if a man believes that he is right
And only he, that no one equals him
In what he says or thinks, he will be found
Empty when searched and tested. Because a man
Even if he be wise, feels no disgrace
In learning many things, in taking care
Not to be over-rigid. You have seen
Trees on the margin of a stream in winter: 660
Those yielding to the flood save every twig,
And those resisting perish root and branch.
So, too, the mariner who never slackens
His taut sheet overturns his craft and spends
Keel uppermost the last part of his voyage.
Let your resentment die. Let yourself change.
For I believe—if I, a younger man,
May have a sound opinion—it is best
That men by nature should be wise in all things.
But most men find they cannot reach that goal;   670
And when this happens, it is also good
To learn to listen to wise counselors.

CHORUS:
　　Sir, when his words are timely, you should heed them.
　　And Haemon, you should profit by his words.
　　Each one of you has spoken reasonably.

CREON:
　　Are men as old as I am to be taught
　　How to behave by men as young as he?

HAEMON:
　　Not to do wrong. If I am young, ignore
　　My youth. Consider only what I do.

CREON:
　　Have you done well in honoring the rebellious?   680

HAEMON:
　　Those who do wrong should not command respect.

CREON:
　　Then that disease has not infected her?

21

HAEMON:
> All of our city with one voice denies it.

CREON:
> Does Thebes give orders for the way I rule?

HAEMON:
> How young you are! How young in saying that!

CREON:
> Am I to govern by another's judgment?

HAEMON:
> A city that is one man's is no city.

CREON:
> A city is the king's. That much is sure.

HAEMON:
> You would rule well in a deserted country.

CREON:
> This boy defends a woman, it appears.   690

HAEMON:
> If you are one. I am concerned for you.

CREON:
> To quarrel with your father does not shame you?

HAEMON:
> Not when I see you failing to do justice.

CREON:
> Am I unjust when I respect my crown?

HAEMON:
> Respect it! When you trample down religion?

CREON:
> Infamous! Giving first place to a woman!

HAEMON:
> But never to anything that would disgrace me.

CREON:
> Each word you utter is a plea for her.

HAEMON:
> For you, too, and for me, and for the gods.

CREON:
> You shall not marry her this side of death.   700

HAEMON:
> Then if she dies, she does not die alone.

CREON:
> What! Has it come to this? You threaten me?

HAEMON:
> No. But I tell you your decree is useless.

CREON:
> You will repent this. You! Teaching me wisdom!

HAEMON:
> I will not call you mad. You are my father.

22

CREON:

    You woman's slave! Your talk will not persuade me.

HAEMON:

    Then what you want is to make all the speeches.

CREON:

    So. Now by all the gods in heaven above us,
    One thing is certain: you are going to pay
    For taunting and insulting me. (*to* ATTENDANTS) Bring out   710
    That hated object. Let her die this moment,
    Here, at her bridegroom's feet, before his eyes.

HAEMON:

    No, you are wrong. Not at my feet. And never
    Will you set eyes upon my face again.
    Rage, rave, with anyone who can bear to listen.

                           Exit HAEMON

CHORUS:

    Sir, he is gone; his anger gives him speed.
    Young men are bitter in their agony.

CREON:

    Let him imagine more than man can do,
    Or let him do more. Never shall he save
    These two girls; they are going to their doom.   720

CHORUS:

    Do you intend to put them both to death?

CREON:

    That was well said. No, not the innocent.

CHORUS:

    And the other? In what way is she to die?

CREON:

    Along a desolate pathway I will lead her,
    And shut her, living, in a rocky vault
    With no more food than will appease the gods,
    So that the city may not be defiled.
    Hades, who is the only god she worships,
    May hear her prayers, and rescue her from death.
    Otherwise she will learn at last, though late,   730
    That to revere the dead is useless toil.

                           Exit CREON

CHORUS:

    None may withstand you, O love unconquered,
      Seizing the wealth of man as your prey,
    In the cheek of a maiden keeping your vigil,
      Till night has faded again to day.
    You roam the wilds to men's farthest dwellings,
      You haunt the boundless face of the sea.
    No god may escape you, no short-lived mortal
      From the madness that love inflicts may flee.

You twist our minds until ruin follows.   740
  The just to unrighteous ways you turn.
You have goaded kinsman to strive with kinsman
  Till the fires of bitter hatred burn.
In the eyes of a bride you shine triumphant;
  Beside the eternal laws your throne
Eternal stands, for great Aphrodite,
  Resistless, works her will on her own.

But now I too am moved. I cannot keep
  Within the bounds of loyalty. I weep
When I behold Antigone, the bride,   750
  Nearing the room where all at last abide.

                              Enter ANTIGONE, *guarded*

ANTIGONE:

        See me, my countrymen! See with what pain
    I tread the path I shall not tread again,
    Looking my last upon the light of day
        That shines for me no more.
    Hades, who gives his sleep to all, me, living, leads away
        To Acheron's dark shore.
    Not mine the hymeneal chant, not mine the bridal song,
        For I, a bride, to Acheron belong.

CHORUS:

        Glorious, therefore, and with praise you tread   760
    The pathway to the deep gulf of the dead.
    You have not felt the force of fate's decrees,
    Struck down by violence, wasted by disease;
    But of your own free will you choose to go,
    Alone of mortals, to the world below.

ANTIGONE:

    I know how sad a death she suffered, she
    Who was our guest here, Phrygian Niobe.
    Stone spread upon her, close as ivy grows,
        And locked her in its chains.
    Now on her wasted form, men say, fall ceaselessly the
                    snows,   770
        Fall ceaselessly the rains;
    While from her grieving eyes drop tears, tears that
                    her bosom steep.
    And like hers, my fate lulls me now to sleep.

CHORUS:

> She was a goddess of the gods' great race;
> Mortals are we and mortal lineage trace.
> But for a woman the renown is great
> In life and death to share a godlike fate.

ANTIGONE:

> By our fathers' gods, I am mocked! I am mocked! Ah! why,
> You men of wealth, do you taunt me before I die?　　　780
> O sacred grove of the city! O waters that flow
> 　From the spring of Dircé! Be witness; to you I cry.
> What manner of woman I am you know
> And by what laws, unloved, unlamented, I go
> 　To my rocky prison, to my unnatural tomb.
> 　　Alas, how ill-bestead!
> No fellowship have I; no others can share my doom,
> Neither mortals nor corpses, neither the quick nor the dead.

CHORUS:

> You have rushed forward with audacious feet
> And dashed yourself against the law's high seat.　　　790
> That was a grievious fall, my child, and yet
> In this ordeal you pay your father's debt.

ANTIGONE:

> You have touched on the heaviest grief that my heart
> 　　　　can hold:
> Grief for my father, sorrow that never grows old
> For our famous house and its doom that the fates have spun.
> 　My mother's bed! Ah! How can its horrors be told?
> My mother who yielded her love to one
> Who was at once my father and her son.
> 　Born of such parents, with them henceforth I abide,
> 　　Wretched, accursed, unwed.　　　800
> 　And you, Polyneices, you found an ill-fated bride,
> And I, the living, am ruined by you, the dead.

CHORUS:

> A pious action may of praise be sure,
> But he who rules a land cannot endure
> An act of disobedience to his rule.
> Your own self-will you have not learned to school.

ANTIGONE:

> Unwept, unfriended, without marriage song,
> Forth on my road I miserable am led;
> 　I may not linger. Not for long

Shall I, most wretched, see the holy sun. 810
My fate no friend bewails, not one;
  For me no tear is shed.

Enter CREON

CREON:

Do you not know that singing and lamentation
Would rise incessantly as death approached,
If they could be of service? Lead her away!
Obey my orders. Shut her in her grave
And leave her there, alone. Then she can take
Her choice of living in that home, or dying.
I am not stained by the guilt of this girl's blood,
But she shall see the light of day no longer. 820

ANTIGONE:

O tomb! O cavern! Everlasting prison!
O bridal-chamber! To you I make my way
To join my kindred, all those who have died
And have been greeted by Persephone.
The last and far most miserable of all,
I seek them now, before I have lived my life.
Yet high are the hopes I cherish that my coming
Will be most welcome to my father; welcome,
Mother, to you; and welcome to you, Brother.
For when you died I ministered to you all, 830
With my own hands washed you and dressed your bodies,
And poured libations at your graves. And now,
Because I have given to you, too, Polyneices,
Such honors as I could, I am brought to this.
And yet all wise men will approve my act.
Not for my children, had I been a mother,
Not for a husband, for his moldering body,
Would I have set myself against the city
As I have done. And the law sanctions me.
Losing a husband, I might find another. 840
I could have other children. But my parents
Are hidden from me in the underworld,
So that no brother's life can bud and bloom
Ever again. And therefore, Polyneices,
I paid you special honor. And for this
Creon has held me guilty of evil-doing,
And leads me captive for my too great boldness.
No bridal bed is mine, no bridal song,
No share in the joys of marriage, and no share
In nursing children and in tending them. 850
But thus afflicted, destitute of friends,

Living, I go down to the vaults of death.
What is the law of heaven that I have broken?
Why should I any longer look to the gods,
Ill-fated as I am? Whose aid should I invoke,
When I for piety am called impious?
If this pleases the gods, then I shall learn
That sin brought death upon me. But if the sin
Lies in my judges, I could wish for them
No harsher fate than they have decreed for me.   860

CHORUS:
    Still the storm rages; still the same gusts blow,
    Troubling her spirit with their savage breath.

CREON:
    Yes. And her guards will pay for being slow.

ANTIGONE:
    Ah! With those words I have drawn close to death.

CREON:
    You cannot hope that you will now be freed
    From the fulfillment of the doom decreed.

ANTIGONE:
    O Thebes, O land of my fathers, O city!
    O gods who begot and guarded my house from of old!
      They seize me, they snatch me away!
      Now, now! They show no pity.   870
      They give no second's delay.
    You elders, you leaders of Thebes, behold me, behold!
      The last of the house of your kings, the last.
      See what I suffer. See the doom
      That is come upon me, and see from whom,
    Because to the laws of heaven I held fast.

                  Exeunt ANTIGONE *and* GUARDS

CHORUS:
    This likewise Danaë endured:
    The light of heaven she changed for a home brass-bound,
      In a tomb-like chamber close immured.
    And yet, O my child, her race was with honor crowned,   880
      And she guarded the seed of Zeus gold-showered.
    But naught from the terrible power of fate is free·
      Neither war, nor city walls high-towered,
    Nor wealth, nor black ships beaten by the sea.

    He too bowed down beneath his doom,
    The son of Dryas, swift-angered Edonian king,
      Shut fast in a rocky prison's gloom.
    How he roused the god with his mad tongue's mocking sting,
      As his frenzy faded, he came to know;

For he sought to make the god-filled maenads mute,   890
   To quench the Bacchic torches' glow,
And angered the Muses, lovers of the flute.

By the double sea and the dark rocks steely blue
   The beach of Bosporus lies and the savage shore
Of Thracian Salmydessus. There the bride
   Of Phineus, whose fierce heart no mercy knew,
Dealt his two sons a blow that for vengeance cried;
   Ares beheld her hand, all stained with gore,
Grasping the pointed shuttle that pierced through
   Their eyes that saw no more.   900

In misery pining, their lot they lamented aloud,
   Sons of a mother whose fortune in marriage was ill.
From the ancient line of Erechtheus her blood she traced;
   Nurtured in caves far-distant and nursed in cloud,
Daughter of Boreas, daughter of gods, she raced
   Swift as a steed on the slope of the soaring hill.
And yet, O child, O child, she also bowed
   To the long-lived fates' harsh will.

Enter TIRESIAS *and* BOY

TIRESIAS:
    Elders of Thebes, we have come to you with one
    Finding for both the pathway that we followed,   910
    For in this fashion must the blind be guided.
CREON:
    What tidings, old Tiresias, are you bringing?
TIRESIAS:
    I will inform you, I the seer. Give heed.
CREON:
    To ignore your counsel has not been my custom.
TIRESIAS:
    Therefore you kept Thebes on a steady course.
CREON:
    I can bear witness to the help you gave.
TIRESIAS:
    Mark this. You stand upon the brink of ruin.
CREON:
    What terrible words are those? What do you mean?
TIRESIAS:
    My meaning is made manifest by my art
    And my art's omens. As I took my station   920
    Upon my ancient seat of augury,
    Where round me birds of every sort come flocking,

I could no longer understand their language.
It was drowned out in a strange, savage clamor,
Shrill, evil, frenzied, inarticulate.
The whirr of wings told me their murderous talons
Tore at each other. Filled with dread, I then
Made trial of burnt sacrifice. The altar
Was fully kindled, but no clear, bright flame
Leaped from the offering; only fatty moisture   930
Oozed from the flesh and trickled on the embers,
Smoking and sputtering. The bladder burst,
And scattered in the air. The folds of fat
Wrapping the thigh-bones melted and left them bare.
Such was the failure of the sacrifice,
That did not yield the sign that I was seeking.
I learned these things from this boy's observation;
He is my guide as I am guide to others.
Your edict brings this suffering to the city,
For every hearth of ours has been defiled   940
And every altar. There the birds and dogs
Have brought their carrion, torn from the corpse
Of ill-starred Polyneices. Hence, the gods
Refuse our prayers, refuse our sacrifice,
Refuse the flame of our burnt-offerings.
No birds cry clearly and auspiciously,
For they are glutted with a slain man's blood.
Therefore, my son, consider what has happened.
All men are liable to grievous error;   950
But he who, having erred, does not remain
Inflexible, but rather makes amends
For ill, is not unwise or unrewarded.
Stubborn self-will incurs the charge of folly.
Give to the fallen the honors he deserves
And do not stab him. Are you being brave
When you inflict new death upon the dead?
Your good I think of; for your good I speak,
And a wise counselor is sweet to hear
When the advice he offers proves of value.

CREON:

Old man, all of you shoot your arrows at me   960
Like archers at a target. You have used
Even the art of prophecy in your plotting.
Long have the tribe of prophets traded in me,
Like a ship's cargo. Drive whatever bargain
May please you, buy, sell, heap up for yourself
Silver of Sardis, gold of India. Yet
I tell you this: that man shall not be buried,

Not though the eagles of Zeus himself should bear
The carrion morsels to their master's throne.
Not even from the dread of such pollution   970
Will I permit his burial, since I know
There is no mortal can defile the gods.
But even the wisest men disastrously
May fall, Tiresias, when for money's sake
They utter shameful words with specious wisdom.

TIRESIAS:
Ah! Do men understand, or even consider—

CREON:
Consider what? Doubtless some platitude!

TIRESIAS:
How precious beyond any wealth is prudence.

CREON:
How full of evil is the lack of prudence.

TIRESIAS:
Yet you are sick, sick with that same disease.   980

CREON:
I will not in reply revile a prophet.

TIRESIAS:
You do. You say my prophecy is false.

CREON:
Well, all the race of seers are mercenary.

TIRESIAS:
And love of base wealth marks the breed of tyrants.

CREON:
Are you aware that you address your King?

TIRESIAS:
I made you King by helping you save Thebes.

CREON:
Wise in your art and vicious in your acts.

TIRESIAS:
Do not enrage me. I should keep my secret.

CREON:
Reveal it. Speak. But do not look for profit.

TIRESIAS:
You too will find no profit in my words.   990

CREON:
How can you earn your pay? I will not change.

TIRESIAS:
Then know this. Yes, be very sure of it.
Only a few more times will you behold
The swift course of the chariot of the sun
Before you give as payment for the dead
Your own dead flesh and blood. For you have thrust

A living soul to darkness, in a tomb
Imprisoned without pity. And a corpse,
Belonging to the gods below you keep
Unpurified, unburied, unrevered.   1000
The dead are no concern either of yours
Or of the gods above, yet you offend them.
So the avengers, the destroyers, Furies
Of Hades and the gods, lurking in ambush,
Wait to inflict your sins upon your head.
Do you still think my tongue is lined with silver?
A time will come, and will not linger coming,
That will awaken in your house the wailing
Of men and women. Hatred shakes the cities,
Hatred of you. Their sons are mangled corpses,   1010
Hallowed with funeral rites by dogs or beasts
Or birds who bear the all-polluting stench
To every city having hearth or altar.
You goaded me, and therefore like an archer
I shoot my angry arrows at your heart,
Sure arrows; you shall not escape their sting.
Boy, lead me home. Let him expend his rage
On younger men, and let him learn to speak
With a more temperate tongue, and school his heart
To feelings finer than his present mood.   1020

Exeunt TIRESIAS *and* BOY

CHORUS:
    Sir, he is gone, with fearful prophecies.
    And from the time that these dark hairs have whitened,
    I have known this: never has he foretold
    Anything that proved false concerning Thebes.

CREON:
    I also know it well, and it dismays me.
    To yield is bitter. But to resist, and bring
    A curse upon my pride is no less bitter.

CHORUS:
    Son of Menoeceus, listen. You must listen.

CREON:
    What should I do? Tell me, I will obey.

CHORUS:
    Go. Free the girl. Release her from the cavern,   1030
    And build a tomb for the man you would not bury.

CREON:
    So that is your advice—that I should yield?

CHORUS:
    Sir, you should not delay. The gods are swift
    In cutting short man's folly with their curse.

CREON:

How hard it is to change! Yet I obey.
I will give up what I had set my heart on.
No one can stand against the blows of fate.

CHORUS:

Go. Go yourself. These things are not for others.

CREON:

I will go this moment. Guards there! All of you!
Take up your axes. Quick! Quick! Over there.   1040
I imprisoned her myself, and I myself
Will set her free. And yet my mind misgives me.
Never to break the ancient law is best.

Exit CREON

CHORUS:

Thou art known by many a name.
O Bacchus! To thee we call.
Cadmean Semele's glory and pride,
Begotten of Zeus, whose terrible lightnings flame,
Whose thunders appall.
Bacchus, thou dost for us all in thy love provide.
Over Icaria thou dost reign,   1050
And where the worshippers journey slow
To the rites of Eleusis, where mountains shield
The multitudes crossing Demeter's welcoming plain.
Thou makest this mother-city of maenads thine own,
A city beside the rippling flow
Of the gentle river, beside the murderous field
Where the teeth of the dragon were sown.

In the torches' wind-blown flare
Thou art seen, in their flicker and smoke.
Where the two-fold peaks of Parnassus gleam,   1060
Corycian nymphs, as they move through the ruddy glare,
Thee, Bacchus, invoke.
They move in their dance beside the Castalian stream.
O Bacchus, guardian divine!
Down from the slopes of Nysa's hills
Where a mantle of ivy covers the ground,
From headlands rich with the purple grape and the vine,
Thou comest to us, thou comest. O be not long!
Thy triumph the echoing city fills.
The streets are loud with thy praises; the highways
resound,   1070
Resound with immortal song.

Thou honorest highly our Theban city,
Thou, and thy mother by lightning slain.

Our people sicken. O Bacchus have pity!
   Across the strait with its moaning wave,
Down from Parnassus, come thou again!
   Come with thy healing feet, and save!

O thou who leadest the stars in chorus,
   Jubilant stars with their breath of fire,
Offspring of Zeus, appear before us!   1080
   Lord of the tumult of night, appear!
With the frenzied dance of thy maenad choir,
   Bacchus, thou giver of good, draw near!

Enter MESSENGER

MESSENGER:
   You of the house of Cadmus and Amphíon,
No man's estate can ever be established
Firmly enough to warrant praise or blame.
Fortune, from day to day, exalts the lucky
And humbles the unlucky. No one knows
Whether his present lot can long endure.
For Creon once was blest, as I count blessings;   1090
He had saved this land of Cadmus from its foes;
He was the sovereign and ruled alone,
The noble father of a royal house.
And now, all has been lost. Because a man
Who has forfeited his joy is not alive,
He is a living corpse. Heap, if you will,
Your house with riches; live in regal pomp.
Yet if your life is unhappy, all these things
Are worth not even the shadow of a vapor
Put in the balance against joy alone.   1100
CHORUS:
   What new disaster has the King's house suffered?
MESSENGER:
   Death. And the guilt of death lies on the living.
CHORUS:
   The guilt of death! Who has been killed? Who killed him?
MESSENGER:
   Haemon is killed, and by no stranger's hand.
CHORUS:
   He killed himself? Or did his father kill him?
MESSENGER:
   He killed himself, enraged by his murderous father.
CHORUS:
   Tiresias! Now your prophecy is fulfilled.

MESSENGER:

Consider, therefore, what remains to do.

CHORUS:

There is the Queen, wretched Eurydice.
Perhaps mere chance has brought her from the palace;   1110
Perhaps she has learned the news about her son.

Enter EURYDICE

EURYDICE:

Thebans, I heard you talking here together
When I was on my way to greet the goddess,
Pallas Athene, and to pray to her.
Just as I loosed the fastening of the door,
The words that told of my calamity
Struck heavily upon my ear. In terror
I fell back fainting in my women's arms.
But now, repeat your story. I shall hear it
As one who is not ignorant of grief.   1120

MESSENGER:

My Lady, I will bear witness to what I saw,
And will omit no syllable of the truth.
Why should I comfort you with words that later
Would prove deceitful? Truth is always best.
Across the plain I guided my Lord Creon
To where unpitied Polyneices lay,
A corpse mangled by dogs. Then we besought
Hecate, goddess of the roads, and Pluto
To moderate their wrath, and to show mercy.
We washed the dead with ceremonial water.   1130
Gathering the scattered fragments that remained,
With fresh-cut boughs we burned them. We heaped up
A mound of native earth above his ashes.
Then we approached the cavern of Death's bride,
The rock-floored marriage-chamber. While as yet
We were far distant, someone heard the sound
Of loud lament in that unhallowed place,
And came to tell our master. As the King
Drew near, there floated through the air a voice,
Faint, indistinct, that uttered a bitter cry.   1140
The King burst out in anguish: 'Can it be
That I, in my misery, have become a prophet?
Will this be the saddest road I ever trod?
My son's voice greets me. Quickly, slaves! Go quickly!
When you have reached the sepulcher, get through
The opening where the stones are wrenched away,
Get to the mouth of the burial chamber. Look,
See if I know his voice—Haemon's, my son's—
Or if I am deluded by the gods.'

We followed our despairing master's bidding   1150
And in the farthest recess of the tomb
We found Antigone, hanging, with her veil
Noosed round her neck. And with her we found Haemon,
His arms flung round her waist, grieving aloud
For his bride lost in death, his ruined marriage,
His father's deeds. But when his father saw him,
Creon cried piteously and going in,
Called to him brokenly: 'My son, my son,
What have you done? What are you thinking of?
What dreadful thing has driven you out of your mind?   1160
Son, come away. I beg you. I beseech you.'
But Haemon glared at him with furious eyes
Instead of answering, spat in his face,
And drew his sword. His father turned to fly
So that he missed his aim. Immediately,
In bitter self-reproach, the wretched boy
Leaned hard against his sword, and drove it deep
Into his side. Then while his life yet lingered,
With failing strength he drew Antigone close;
And as he lay there gasping heavily,   1170
Over her white cheek his blood ebbed away.
The dead lie clasped together. He is wedded,
Not in this world but in the house of Death.
He has borne witness that of all the evils
Afflicting man, the worst is lack of wisdom.

Exit EURYDICE

CHORUS:
What does that mean? Who can interpret it?
The Queen has gone without a single word.

MESSENGER:
It startles me. And yet I hope it means
That hearing these dreadful things about her son,
She will not let herself show grief in public   1180
But will lament in private with her women.
Schooled in discretion, she will do no wrong.

CHORUS:
How can we tell? Surely too great a silence
Is no less ominous than too loud lament.

MESSENGER:
Then I will enter. Perhaps she is concealing
Some secret purpose in her passionate heart.
I will find out, for you are right in saying
Too great a silence may be ominous.

Exit MESSENGER. *Enter* CREON *with* ATTENDANTS,
carrying the body of HAEMON *on a bier*

CHORUS:

> Thebans, look there! The King himself draws near,
> Bearing a load whose tale is all too clear. 1190
> This is a work—if we dare speak our thought—
> That not another's but his own hands wrought.

CREON:

> O, how may my sin be told?
> The stubborn, death-fraught sin of a darkened brain!
>   Behold us here, behold
> Father and son, the slayer and the slain!
>   Pain, only pain
> Has come of my design.
>   Fate struck too soon; too soon your spirit fled.
>   My son, my young son, you are lying dead 1200
> Not for your folly, but for mine, for mine.

CHORUS:

> Sir, you have come to learn the right too late.

CREON:

> My lesson has been bitter and complete.
> Some god has struck me down with crushing weight,
> Filling my heart with cruelty and hate,
>   Trampling my happiness beneath his feet.
>   Grief, bitter grief, is man's fate.

Enter MESSENGER

MESSENGER (*indicating* HAEMON):

> Your load is heavy, Sir, but there is more.
> That is the burden you are bearing now.
> Soon you must bear new woe within your house. 1210

CREON:

> And what worse misery can follow this?

MESSENGER:

> Your wife is dead, a mother like her son.
> Poor woman, by her own hand she has died.

CREON:

> By her own hand she died.
> Death, spare me! Can you never have your fill?
>   Never be satisfied?
> Herald of evil, messenger of ill,
>   Your harsh words kill,
> They smite me now anew.
>   My wife is dead—You tell me my wife is dead. 1220
>   Death after death is heaped upon my head.
> Speak to me, boy. Is what you tell me true?

MESSENGER:
    It is no longer hidden. Sir, look there.
                (*The body of* EURYDICE *is disclosed*
                through the palace doors)

CREON:
    Another horror that makes blind mine eyes!
    What further agony has fate in store?
    My dead son's body in my arms I bore,
      And now beside him his dead mother lies.
        I can endure no more.

MESSENGER:
    There at the altar with a keen-edged knife
    She stabbed herself; and as her eyes were darkened,   1230
    She wailed the death of Megareus, her son,
    Who earlier had met a noble fate;
    She wailed for Haemon; then, with her last breath,
    You, as the slayer of your sons, she cursed.

CREON:
    I am shaken with terror, with terror past belief.
    Is there none here to end my anguish? None?
      No sword to pierce me? Broken with my grief,
    So steeped in agony that we are one.

MESSENGER:
    Sir, as she died, she burdened you with guilt,
    Charging you with the death of both your sons.   1240

CREON:
    And by what act of violence did she die?

MESSENGER:
    Hearing the shrill lament for Haemon's fate,
    Deep in her heart she drove the bright blade home.

CREON (*to* HAEMON):
    I am your slayer, I alone.
    I am guilty, only I.
      I, and none other, must atone.
    Lead me away. The truth I own.
      Nothing is left, except to die.

CHORUS:
    If anything can be good, those words are good.
    For when calamity has come upon us,   1250
    The thing that is the briefest is the best.

CREON:
    Draw near me, death! O longed for death, draw near!
    Most welcome destiny, make no delay.
      Tell me my last hour, my last breath, is here.
    I have no wish to see another day.

CHORUS:

> Such things are yet to come. We are concerned
> With doing what must needs be done today.
> The future rests in other hands than ours.

CREON:

> That is my whole desire. That is my prayer.

CHORUS:

> No. Do not pray. Men must accept their doom. 1260

CREON:

> My life's work there before me lies.
> My folly slew my wife, my son.
> I know not where to turn mine eyes.
> All my misdeeds before me rise.
> Lead me away, brought low, undone.

Exit CREON

CHORUS:

> The crown of happiness is to be wise.
> Honor the gods, and the gods' edicts prize.
> They strike down boastful men and men grown bold.
> Wisdom we learn at last, when we are old.

Oedipus the King

CHARACTERS IN THE PLAY

OEDIPUS, *King of Thebes*

JOCASTA, *Queen of Thebes, wife and mother of* OEDIPUS

CREON, *brother of* JOCASTA

TIRESIAS, *a prophet*

BOY, *attendant of* TIRESIAS

PRIEST OF ZEUS

SHEPHERD

FIRST MESSENGER, *from Corinth*

SECOND MESSENGER

CHORUS *of Theban elders*

ATTENDANTS

OEDIPUS THE KING

SCENE: *Before the doors of the palace of* OEDIPUS *at Thebes.
A crowd of citizens are seated next to the two altars
at the sides. In front of one of the altars stands the*
PRIEST OF ZEUS.

Enter OEDIPUS

OEDIPUS:

Why are you here as suppliants, my children,
You in whose veins the blood of Cadmus flows?
What is the reason for your boughs of olive,
The fumes of incense, the laments and prayers
That fill the city? Because I thought it wrong,
My children, to depend on what was told me,
I have come to you myself, I, Oedipus,
Renowned in the sight of all. (*to* PRIEST) Tell me—you are
Their natural spokesman—what desire or fear
Brings you before me? I will gladly give you   10
Such help as is in my power. It would be heartless
Not to take pity on a plea like this.

PRIEST:

King Oedipus, you see us, young and old,
Gathered about your altars: some, mere fledglings
Not able yet to fly; some, bowed with age;
Some, priests, and I the priest of Zeus among them;
And these, who are the flower of our young manhood.
The rest of us are seated—the whole city—
With our wreathed branches in the market places,
Before the shrines of Pallas, before the fire   20
By which we read the auguries of Apollo.
Thebes, as you see yourself, is overwhelmed
By the waves of death that break upon her head.
No fruit comes from her blighted buds; her cattle
Die in the fields; her wives bring forth dead children.
A hideous pestilence consumes the city,
Striking us down like a god armed with fire,
Emptying the house of Cadmus, filling full
The dark of Hades with loud lamentation.
I and these children have not thronged your altars   30
Because we hold you equal to the immortals,
But because we hold you foremost among men,

41

Both in the happenings of daily life
And when some visitation of the gods
Confronts us. For we know that when you came here,
You freed us from our bondage, the bitter tribute
The Sphinx wrung from us by her sorceries.
And we know too that you accomplished this
Without foreknowledge, or clue that we could furnish.
We think, indeed, some god befriended you, 40
When you renewed our lives. Therefore, great king,
Glorious in all men's eyes, we now beseech you
To find some way of helping us, your suppliants,
Some way the gods themselves have told you of,
Or one that lies within our mortal power;
For the words of men experienced in evil
Are mighty and effectual. Oedipus!
Rescue our city and preserve your honor,
Since the land hails you as her savior now
For your past service. Never let us say 50
That when you ruled us, we were lifted up
Only to be thrown down. Restore the state
And keep it forever steadfast. Bring again
The happiness and good fortune you once brought us.
If you are still to reign as you reign now,
Then it is better to have men for subjects
Than to be king of a mere wilderness,
Since neither ship nor town has any value
Without companions or inhabitants.

OEDIPUS:

I pity you, my children. Well I know 60
What hopes have brought you here, and well I know
That all of you are suffering. Yet your grief,
However great, is not so great as mine.
Each of you suffers for himself alone,
But my heart feels the heaviness of my sorrow,
Your sorrow, and the sorrow of all the others.
You have not roused me, I have not been sleeping.
No. I have wept, wept long and bitterly,
Treading the devious paths of anxious thought;
And I have taken the only hopeful course 70
That I could find. I have sent my kinsman, Creon,
Son of Menoeceus, to the Pythian home
Of Phoebus Apollo to find what word or deed
Of mine might save the city. He has delayed
Too long already, his absence troubles me;
But when he comes, I pledge myself to do
My utmost to obey the god's command.

PRIEST:

Your words are timely, for even as you speak
They sign to me that Creon is drawing near.

OEDIPUS:

O Lord Apollo! Grant he may bring to us   80
Fortune as smiling as his smiling face.

PRIEST:

Surely he brings good fortune. Look! The crown
Of bay leaves that he wears is full of berries.

OEDIPUS:

We shall know soon, for he is close enough
To hear us. Brother, son of Monoeceus, speak!
What news? What news do you bring us from the god?

Enter CREON

CREON:

Good news. If we can find the fitting way
To end this heavy scourge, all will be well.

OEDIPUS:

That neither gives me courage nor alarms me.
What does the god say? What is the oracle?   90

CREON:

If you wish me to speak in public, I will do so.
Otherwise let us go in and speak alone.

OEDIPUS:

Speak here before everyone. I feel more sorrow
For their sakes than I feel for my own life.

CREON:

Then I will give the message of Lord Phoebus:
A plain command to drive out the pollution
Here in our midst, and not to nourish it
Till our disease has grown incurable.

OEDIPUS:

What rite will purge us? How are we corrupted?

CREON:

We must banish a man, or have him put to death   100
To atone for the blood he shed, for it is blood
That has brought this tempest down upon the city.

OEDIPUS:

Who is the victim whose murder is revealed?

CREON:

King Laius, who was our lord before you came
To steer the city on its proper course.

OEDIPUS:

I know his name well, but I never saw him.

CREON:

> Laius was killed, and now we are commanded
> To punish his killers, whoever they may be.

OEDIPUS:

> How can they be discovered? Where shall we look
> For the faint traces of this ancient crime? 110

CREON:

> In Thebes, the god said. Truth can be always found:
> Only what is neglected ever escapes.

OEDIPUS:

> Where was King Laius murdered? In his home,
> Out in the fields, or in some foreign land?

CREON:

> He told us he was journeying to Delphi.
> After he left, he was never seen again.

OEDIPUS:

> Was no one with King Laius who saw what happened?
> You could have put his story to good use.

CREON:

> The sole survivor fled from the scene in terror,
> And there was only one thing he was sure of. 120

OEDIPUS:

> What was it? A clue might lead us far
> Which gave us even the faintest glimmer of hope.

CREON:

> He said that they were violently attacked
> Not by one man but by a band of robbers.

OEDIPUS:

> Robbers are not so daring. Were they bribed
> To commit this crime by some one here in Thebes?

CREON:

> That was suspected. But in our time of trouble
> No one appeared to avenge the death of Laius.

OEDIPUS:

> But your King was killed! What troubles could you have had
> To keep you from searching closely for his killers? 130

CREON:

> We had the Sphinx. Her riddle made us turn
> From mysteries to what lay before our doors.

OEDIPUS:

> Then I will start fresh and again make clear
> Things that are dark. All honor to Apollo
> And to you, Creon, for acting as you have done
> On the dead King's behalf. So I will take
> My rightful place beside you as your ally,
> Avenging Thebes and bowing to the god.

Not for a stranger will I dispel this taint,
But for my own sake, since the murderer,   140
Whoever he is, may strike at me as well.
Therefore in helping Laius I help myself.
Come, children, come! Rise from the altar steps,
And carry away those branches. Summon here
The people of Cadmus. Tell them I mean to leave
Nothing undone. So with Apollo's aid
We may at last be saved—or meet destruction.

Exit OEDIPUS

PRIEST:

My children, let us go. The King has promised
The favor that we sought. And may Lord Phoebus
Come to us with his oracles, assuage   150
Our misery, and deliver us from death.

Exeunt. Enter CHORUS

CHORUS:

The god's great word, in whose sweetness we ever rejoice,
        To our glorious city is drawing nigh,
Now, even now, from the gold of the Delphic shrine.
        What next decree will be thine,
Apollo, thou healer, to whom in our dread we cry?
        We are anguished, racked, and beset by fears!
What fate will be ours? One fashioned for us alone,
        Or one that in ancient time was known
        That returns once more with the circling years?   160
Child of our golden hope, O speak, thou immortal voice!

Divine Athene, daughter of Zeus, O hear!
        Hear thou, Artemis! Thee we hail,
Our guardian goddess throned in the market place.
        Apollo, we ask thy grace.
Shine forth, all three, and the menace of death will fail.
        Answer our call! Shall we call in vain?
If ever ye came in the years that have gone before,
        Return, and save us from plague once more,
        Rescue our city from fiery pain!   170
Be your threefold strength our shield. Draw near to us now, draw near!

Death is upon us. We bear a burden of bitter grief.
There is nothing can save us now, no device that our thought can frame.
        No blossom, no fruit, no harvest sheaf
        Springs from the blighted and barren earth.
Women cry out in travail and bring no children to birth;
        But swift as a bird, swift as the sweep of flame,

Life after life takes sudden flight
To the western god, to the last, dark shore of night.

Ruin has fallen on Thebes. Without number her children are
    dead;   180
Unmourned, unattended, unpitied, they lie polluting the ground.
 Grey-haired mothers and wives new-wed
 Wail at the altars everywhere,
With entreaty, with loud lament, with clamor filling the air.
 And songs of praise to Apollo, the healer, resound.
 Athene, thou knowest our desperate need.
Lend us thy strength. Give heed to our prayer, give heed!

Fierce Ares has fallen upon us. He comes unarrayed for war,
Yet he fills our ears with shrieking, he folds us in fiery death.
 Grant that he soon may turn in headlong flight from our land, 190
Swept to the western deep by the fair wind's favoring breath,
 Or swept to the savage sea that washes the Thracian shore,
We few who escape the night are stricken down in the day.
 O Zeus, whose bolts of thunder are balanced within thy hand,
Hurl down thy lightning upon him! Father, be swift to slay!

Save us, light-bringing Phoebus! The shower of thine arrows let fly;
Loose them, triumphant and swift, from the golden string of thy bow!
 O goddess, his radiant sister, roaming the Lycian glade,
Come with the flash of thy fire! Artemis, conquer our foe!
 And thou, O wine-flushed god to whom the Bacchantes cry, 200
With thy brilliant torch ablaze amid shouts of thy maenad train,
 With thy hair enwreathed with gold, O Bacchus, we beg thine aid
Against our destroyer Ares, the god whom the gods disdain!

Enter OEDIPUS

OEDIPUS:
  You have been praying. If you heed my words
  And seek the remedy for your own disease,
  The gods will hear your prayers, and you will find
  Relief and comfort. I myself know nothing
  About this story, nothing about the murder,
  So that unaided and without a clue
  I could not have tracked it down for any distance. 210
  And because I have only recently been received
  Among you as a citizen, to you all,
  And to all the rest, I make this proclamation:
  Whoever knows the man who killed King Laius,
  Let him declare his knowledge openly.

If he himself is guilty, let him confess
And go unpunished, except for banishment.
Or if he knows the murderer was an alien,
Let him by speaking earn his due reward,
And thanks as well. But if he holds his tongue,   220
Hoping to save himself or save a friend,
Then let him hear what I, the King, decree
For all who live in Thebes, the land I rule.
No one shall give this murderer shelter. No one
Shall speak to him. No one shall let him share
In sacrifice or prayer or lustral rites.
The door of every house is barred against him.
The god has shown me that he is polluted.
So by this edict I ally myself
With Phoebus and the slain. As for the slayer,   230
Whether he had accomplices or not,
This is my solemn prayer concerning him:
May evil come of evil; may he live
A wretched life and meet a wretched end.
And as for me, if I should knowingly
Admit him as a member of my household,
May the same fate which I invoked for others
Fall upon me. Make my words good, I charge you,
For love of me, Apollo, and our country
Blasted by the displeasure of the gods.   240
You should not have left this guilt unpurified,
Even without an oracle to urge you,
When a man so noble, a man who was your King,
Had met his death. Rather, it was your duty
To seek the truth. But now, since it is I
Who hold the sovereignty that once was his,
I who have wed his wife, who would have been
Bound to him by the tie of having children
Born of one mother, if he had had a child
To be a blessing, if fate had not struck him down—   250
Since this is so, I intend to fight his battle
As though he were my father. I will leave
Nothing undone to find his murderer,
Avenging him and all his ancestors.
And I pray the gods that those who disobey
May suffer. May their fields bring forth no harvest,
Their wives no children; may the present plague,
Or one yet worse, consume them. But as for you,
All of you citizens who are loyal to me,
May Justice, our champion, and all the gods   260
Show you their favor in the days to come.

CHORUS:

> King Oedipus, I will speak to avoid your curse.
> I am no slayer, nor can I point him out.
> The question came to us from Phoebus Apollo;
> It is for him to tell us who is guilty.

OEDIPUS:

> Yes. But no man on earth is strong enough
> To force the gods to act against their will.

CHORUS:

> There is, I think, a second course to follow.

OEDIPUS:

> If there is yet a third, let me know that.

CHORUS:

> Tiresias, the prophet, has the clearest vision   270
> Next to our Lord Apollo. He is the man
> Who can do most to help us in our search.

OEDIPUS:

> I have not forgotten. Creon suggested it,
> And I have summoned him, summoned him twice.
> I am astonished he is not here already.

CHORUS:

> The only rumors are old and half-forgotten.

OEDIPUS:

> What are they? I must find out all I can.

CHORUS:

> It is said the King was killed by travelers.

OEDIPUS:

> So I have heard, but there is no eye-witness.

CHORUS:

> If fear can touch them, they will reveal themselves   280
> Once they have heard so dreadful a curse as yours.

OEDIPUS:

> Murderers are not terrified by words.

CHORUS:

> But they can be convicted by the man
> Being brought here now, Tiresias. He alone
> Is godlike in his knowledge of the truth.

Enter TIRESIAS, *led by a* BOY

OEDIPUS:

> You know all things in heaven and earth, Tiresias:
> Things you may speak of openly, and secrets
> Holy and not to be revealed. You know,
> Blind though you are, the plague that ruins Thebes.
> And you, great prophet, you alone can save us.   290

Phoebus has sent an answer to our question,
An answer that the messengers may have told you,
Saying there was no cure for our condition
Until we found the killers of King Laius
And banished them or had them put to death.
Therefore, Tiresias, do not begrudge your skill
In the voice of birds or other prophecy,
But save yourself, save me, save the whole city,
Save everything that the pestilence defiles.
We are at your mercy, and man's noblest task   300
Is to use all his powers in helping others.

TIRESIAS:

How dreadful a thing, how dreadful a thing is wisdom,
When to be wise is useless! This I knew
But I forgot, or else I would never have come.

OEDIPUS:

What is the matter? Why are you so troubled?

TIRESIAS:

Oedipus, let me go home. Then you will bear
Your burden, and I mine, more easily.

OEDIPUS:

Custom entitles us to hear your message.
By being silent you harm your native land.

TIRESIAS:

You do not know when, and when not to speak.   310
Silence will save me from the same misfortune.

OEDIPUS:

If you can be of help, then all of us
Kneel and implore you not to turn away.

TIRESIAS:

I refuse to pain you. I refuse to pain myself.
It is useless to ask me. I will tell you nothing.

OEDIPUS:

You utter scoundrel! You would enrage a stone!
Is there no limit to your stubbornness?

TIRESIAS:

You blame my anger and forget your own.

OEDIPUS:

No one could help being angry when he heard
How you dishonor and ignore the state.   320

TIRESIAS:

What is to come will come, though I keep silent.

OEDIPUS:

If it must come, your duty is to speak.

TIRESIAS:

I will say no more. Rage to your heart's content.

OEDIPUS:

Rage? Yes, I will rage! I will spare you nothing.
In the plot against King Laius, I have no doubt
That you were an accomplice, yes, almost
The actual killer. If you had not been blind,
I would have said that you alone were guilty.

TIRESIAS:

Then listen to my command! Obey the edict
That you yourself proclaimed and never speak,   330
From this day on, to me or any Theban.
You are the sinner who pollutes our land.

OEDIPUS:

Have you no shame? How do you hope to escape
The consequence of such an accusation?

TIRESIAS:

I have escaped. My strength is the living truth.

OEDIPUS:

This is no prophecy. Who taught you this?

TIRESIAS:

You did. You forced me to speak against my will.

OEDIPUS:

Repeat your slander. Let me learn it better.

TIRESIAS:

Are you trying to tempt me into saying more?
I have spoken already. Have you not understood?   340

OEDIPUS:

No, not entirely. Give your speech again.

TIRESIAS:

I say you are the killer, you yourself.

OEDIPUS:

Twice the same insult! You will pay for it.

TIRESIAS:

Shall I say more to make you still more angry?

OEDIPUS:

Say what you want to. It will make no sense.

TIRESIAS:

You are living in shame with those most dear to you,
As yet in ignorance of your dreadful fate.

OEDIPUS:

Do you suppose that you can always use
Language like that and not be punished for it?

TIRESIAS:

Yes. I am safe, if truth has any strength.   350

OEDIPUS:

Truth can save anyone excepting you,
You with no eyes, no hearing, and no brains!

TIRESIAS:

    Poor fool! You taunt me, but you soon will hear
    The self-same insults heaped upon your head.

OEDIPUS:

    You live in endless night. What can you do
    To me or anyone else who sees the day?

TIRESIAS:

    Nothing. I have no hand in your destruction.
    For that, Apollo needs no help from me.

OEDIPUS:

    Apollo! Is this your trick, or is it Creon's?

TIRESIAS:

    Creon is guiltless. The evil is in you.   360

OEDIPUS:

    How great is the envy roused by wealth, by kingship,
    By the subtle skill that triumphs over others
    In life's hard struggle! Creon, who has been
    For years my trusted friend, has stealthily
    Crept in upon me anxious to seize my power,
    The unsought gift the city freely gave me.
    Anxious to overthrow me, he has bribed
    This scheming mountebank, this fraud, this trickster,
    Blind in his art and in everything but money!
    Your art of prophecy! When have you shown it?   370
    Not when the watch-dog of the gods was here,
    Chanting her riddle. Why did you say nothing,
    When you might have saved the city? Yet her puzzle
    Could not be solved by the first passer-by.
    A prophet's skill was needed, and you proved
    That you had no such skill, either in birds
    Or any other means the gods have given.
    But I came, I, the ignorant Oedipus,
    And silenced her. I had no birds to help me.
    I used my brains. And it is I you now   380
    Are trying to destroy in the hope of standing
    Close beside Creon's throne. You will regret
    This zeal of yours to purify the land,
    You and your fellow-plotter. You seem old;
    Otherwise you would pay for your presumption.

CHORUS:

    Sir, it appears to us that both of you
    Have spoken in anger. Anger serves no purpose.
    Rather we should consider in what way
    We best can carry out the god's command.

TIRESIAS:

King though you are, I have a right to answer   390
Equal to yours. In that I too am king.
I serve Apollo. I do not acknowledge
You as my lord or Creon as my patron.
You have seen fit to taunt me with my blindness.
Therefore I tell you this: you have your eyesight
And cannot see the sin of your existence,
Cannot see where you live or whom you live with,
Are ignorant of your parents, bring disgrace
Upon your kindred in the world below
And here on earth. And soon the double lash   400
Of your mother's and father's curse will drive you headlong
Out of the country, blinded, with your cries
Heard everywhere, echoed by every hill
In all Cithaeron. Then you will have learned
The meaning of your marriage, learned in what harbor,
After so fair a voyage, you were shipwrecked.
And other horrors you could never dream of
Will teach you who you are, will drag you down
To the level of your children. Heap your insults
On Creon and my message if you choose to.   410
Still no one ever will endure the weight
Of greater misery than will fall on you.

OEDIPUS:

Am I supposed to endure such talk as this,
Such talk from him? Go, curse you, go! Be quick!

TIRESIAS:

Except for your summons I would never have come.

OEDIPUS:

And I would never have sent for you so soon
If I had known you would prove to be a fool.

TIRESIAS:

Yes. I have proved a fool—in your opinion,
And yet your parents thought that I was wise.

OEDIPUS:

What parents? Wait! Who was my father? Tell me!   420

TIRESIAS:

Today will see your birth and your destruction.

OEDIPUS:

You cannot speak unless you speak in riddles!

TIRESIAS:

And yet how brilliant you are in solving them!

OEDIPUS:

You sneer at me for what has made me great.

TIRESIAS:

The same good fortune that has ruined you.

OEDIPUS:
> If I have saved the city, nothing else matters.

TIRESIAS:
> In that case I will go. Boy, take me home.

OEDIPUS:
> Yes, let him take you. Here, you are in the way.
> Once you are gone, you will give no further trouble.

TIRESIAS:
> I will not go before I have said my say,   430
> Indifferent to your black looks. You cannot harm me.
> And I say this: the man whom you have sought,
> Whom you have threatened, whom you have proclaimed
> The killer of King Laius—he is here.
> Now thought an alien, he shall prove to be
> A native Theban, to his deep dismay.
> Now he has eyesight, now his wealth is great;
> But he shall make his way to foreign soil
> Blinded, in beggary, groping with a stick.
> In his own household he shall be shown to be   440
> The father of his children—and their brother,
> Son to the woman who bore him—and her husband,
> The killer and the bedfellow of his father.
> Go and consider this; and if you find
> That I have been mistaken, you can say
> That I have lost my skill in prophecy.

> *Exeunt* OEDIPUS *and* TIRESIAS

CHORUS:

> What man is this the god from the Delphic rock denounces,
>> Whose deeds are too shameful to tell, whose murderous hands
>>> are red?
> Let his feet be swifter now than hooves of horses racing
>> The storm-clouds overhead.   450
> For Zeus's son, Apollo, leaps in anger upon him,
>> Armed with lightning to strike and slay;
> And the terrible Fates, unflagging, relentless,
>> Follow the track of their prey.

> The words of the god have flashed from the peaks of snowy Parnassus,
>> Commanding us all to seek this killer as yet unknown.
> Deep in the tangled woods, through rocks and caves he is roaming
>> Like a savage bull, alone.
> On his lonely path he journeys, wretched, broken by sorrow,
>> Seeking to flee from the fate he fears;   460
> But the voice from the center of earth that doomed him
>> Inescapably rings in his ears.

53

Dreadful, dreadful those words! We can neither approve nor
    deny them.
  Shaken, confounded with fears, we know not what to say.
Nothing is clear to us, nothing—what is to come tomorrow,
    Or what is upon us today.
If the prophet seeks revenge for the unsolved murder of Laius,
    Why is Oedipus charged with crime?
  Because some deep-rooted hate divides their royal houses?
  The houses of Laius and Oedipus, son of the King of Corinth?   470
    There is none that we know of, now, or in ancient time.

From Zeus's eyes and Apollo's no human secret is hidden;
  But man has no test for truth, no measure his wit can devise.
Tiresias, indeed, excels in every art of his office,
    And yet we too may be wise.
Though Oedipus stands accused, until he is proven guilty
    We cannot blacken his name;
  For he showed his wisdom the day the wingéd maiden faced him.
He triumphed in that ordeal, saved us, and won our affection.
  We can never believe he stooped to an act of shame.   480

Enter CREON

CREON:
    Thebans, I come here outraged and indignant,
    For I have learned that Oedipus has accused me
    Of dreadful crimes. If, in the present crisis,
    He thinks that I have wronged him in any way,
    Wronged him in word or deed, then let my life
    Come to a speedy close. I cannot bear
    The burden of such scandal. The attack
    Ruins me utterly, if my friends, and you,
    And the whole city are to call me traitor.

CHORUS:
    Perhaps his words were only a burst of anger,   490
    And were not meant as a deliberate insult.

CREON:
    He *did* say that I plotted with Tiresias?
    And that the prophet lied at my suggestion?

CHORUS:
    Those were his words. I cannot guess his motive.

CREON:
    Were his eyes clear and steady? Was his mind
    Unclouded, when he brought this charge against me?

CHORUS:
    I cannot say. To see what princes do
    Is not our province. Here comes the King himself.

Enter OEDIPUS

OEDIPUS:

So you are here! What brought you to my door?
Impudence? Insolence? You, my murderer!   500
You, the notorious stealer of my crown!
Why did you hatch this plot? What kind of man,
By heaven, what kind of man, could you have thought me?
A coward or a fool? Did you suppose
I would not see your trickery take shape,
Or when I saw it, would not counter it?
How stupid you were to reach for royal power
Without a troop of followers or rich friends!
Only a mob and money win a kingdom.

CREON:

Sir, let me speak. When you have heard my answer,   510
You will have grounds on which to base your judgment.

OEDIPUS:

I cannot follow all your clever talk.
I only know that you are dangerous.

CREON:

That is the issue. Let me explain that first.

OEDIPUS:

Do not explain that you are true to me.

CREON:

If you imagine that a blind self-will
Is strength of character, you are mistaken.

OEDIPUS:

As you are, if you strike at your own house,
And then expect to escape all punishment.

CREON:

Yes, you are right. That would be foolishness.   520
But tell me, what have I done? How have I harmed you?

OEDIPUS:

Did you, or did you not, urge me to summon
Tiresias, that revered, that holy prophet?

CREON:

Yes. And I still think my advice was good.

OEDIPUS:

Then answer this: how long ago was Laius—

CREON:

Laius! Why how am I concerned with him?

OEDIPUS:

How many years ago was Laius murdered?

CREON:

So many they cannot easily be counted.

OEDIPUS:

And was Tiresias just as cunning then?

CREON:

As wise and honored as he is today.   530

OEDIPUS:

At that time did he ever mention me?

CREON:

Not in my hearing. I am sure of that.

OEDIPUS:

And the murderer—a thorough search was made?

CREON:

Yes, certainly, but we discovered nothing.

OEDIPUS:

Then why did the man of wisdom hold his tongue?

CREON:

I cannot say. Guessing is not my habit.

OEDIPUS:

One thing at least you need not guess about.

CREON:

What is it? If I know it, I will tell you.

OEDIPUS:

Tiresias would not have said I murdered Laius,
If you two had not put your heads together.   540

CREON:

You best know what he said. But now I claim
The right to take my turn in asking questions.

OEDIPUS:

Very well, ask. You never can find me guilty.

CREON:

Then answer this: my sister is your wife?

OEDIPUS:

I cannot deny that fact. She is my wife.

CREON:

And in your rule she has an equal share?

OEDIPUS:

She has no wish that goes unsatisfied.

CREON:

And as the third I stand beside you both?

OEDIPUS:

True. That position proves your treachery.

CREON:

No. You would see, if you thought the matter through   550
As I have done. Consider. Who would choose
Kingship and all the terrors that go with it,
If, with the same power, he could sleep in peace?
I have no longing for a royal title
Rather than royal freedom. No, not I,

Nor any moderate man. Now I fear nothing.
Every request I make of you is granted,
And yet as king I should have many duties
That went against the grain. Then how could rule
Be sweeter than untroubled influence?   560
I have not lost my mind. I want no honors
Except the ones that bring me solid good.
Now all men welcome me and wish me joy.
Now all your suitors ask to speak with me,
Knowing they cannot otherwise succeed.
Why should I throw away a life like this
For a king's life? No one is treacherous
Who knows his own best interests. To conspire
With other men, or to be false myself,
Is not my nature. Put me to the test.   570
First, go to Delphi. Ask if I told the truth
About the oracle. Then if you find
I have had dealings with Tiresias, kill me.
My voice will echo yours in passing sentence.
But base your verdict upon something more
Than mere suspicion. Great injustice comes
From random judgments that bad men are good
And good men bad. To throw away a friend
Is, in effect, to throw away your life,
The prize you treasure most. All this, in time,   580
Will become clear to you, for time alone
Proves a man's honesty, but wickedness
Can be discovered in a single day.

CHORUS:

Sir, that is good advice, if one is prudent.
Hasty decisions always lead to danger.

OEDIPUS:

When a conspiracy is quick in forming,
I must move quickly to retaliate.
If I sat still and let my enemy act,
I would lose everything that he would gain.

CREON:

So then, my banishment is what you want?   590

OEDIPUS:

No, not your banishment. Your execution.

CREON:

I think you are mad.   OE.: I can protect myself.

CREON:

You should protect me also.   OE.: You? A traitor?

CREON:

Suppose you are wrong?   OE.: I am the King. I rule.

CREON:

> Not if you rule unjustly. OE.: Thebes! Hear that!

CREON:

> Thebes is my city too, as well as yours.

CHORUS:

> No more, no more, sirs! Here is Queen Jocasta.
> She comes in time to help make peace between you.

Enter JOCASTA

JOCASTA:

> Oedipus! Creon! How can you be so foolish?
> What! Quarrel now about a private matter   600
> When the land is dying? You should be ashamed.
> Come, Oedipus, come in. Creon, go home.
> You make a trivial problem too important.

CREON:

> Sister, your husband has made dreadful threats.
> He claims the right to have me put to death
> Or have me exiled. He need only choose.

OEDIPUS:

> Yes. I have caught him at his treachery,
> Plotting against the person of the King.

CREON:

> If I am guilty, may it be my fate
> To live in misery and to die accursed.   610

JOCASTA:

> Believe him, Oedipus, believe him, spare him—
> I beg you by the gods—for his oath's sake,
> For my sake, for the sake of all men here.

CHORUS:

> Consent, O King. Be gracious. Hear us, we beg you.

OEDIPUS: What shall I hear? To what shall I consent?

CHORUS: Respect the evidence of Creon's wisdom,
> Respect the oath of innocence he has taken.

OE.: You know what this means? CH.: Yes. OE.: Tell me again what
> you ask for.

CHORUS: To yield, to relent.
> He is your friend and swears he is not guilty.   620
> Do not act in haste, convicting him out of hand.

OEDIPUS: When you ask for this, you ask for my destruction;
> You sentence me to death or to banishment.
> Be sure that you understand.

CHORUS:
>   No, by Apollo, no!
>   If such a thought has ever crossed my mind,
>   Then may I never find
>   A friend to love me or a god to save;
>   And may dark doom pursue me to the grave.
>   My country perishes, and now new woe   630
>   Springs from your quarrel, one affliction more
>   Has come upon us, and my heart is sore.

OEDIPUS:
>   Let him go free, even though that destroys me.
>   I shall be killed, or exiled in disgrace.
>   Not his appeal but yours aroused my pity.
>   I shall hate him always, no matter where he is.

CREON:
>   You go beyond all bounds when you are angry,
>   And are sullen when you yield. Natures like yours
>   Inflict their heaviest torments on themselves.

OEDIPUS:
>   Go! Go! Leave me in peace! CR.: Yes, I will go.   640
>   You have not understood, but in the sight
>   Of all these men here I am innocent.

>   *Exit* CREON

CHORUS: Take the King with you, Madam, to the palace.
JOCASTA: When I have learned what happened, we will go.
CHORUS: The King was filled with fear and blind suspicion.
>   Creon resented what he thought injustice.
JOC.:   Both were at fault? CH.: Both. JOC.: Why was the King
>   suspicious?
CHORUS: Do not seek to know.
>   We have said enough. In a time of pain and trouble
>   Inquire no further. Let the matter rest.   650
OEDIPUS: Your well meant pleading turned me from my purpose,
>   And now you come to this. You fall so low
>   As to think silence best.

CHORUS:
>   I say again, O King,
>   No one except a madman or a fool
>   Would throw aside your rule.
>   For you delivered us; your single hand

59

Lifted the load from our belovéd land.
　When we were mad with grief and suffering,
In our extremity you found a way　　　　　　　　　660
　To save the city, as you will today.

JOCASTA:

But tell *me*, Oedipus, tell *me*, I beg you,
Why you were so unyielding in your anger.

OEDIPUS:

I will, Jocasta, for I honor you
More than I do the elders. It was Creon's plotting.

JOCASTA:

What do you mean? What was your accusation?

OEDIPUS:

He says I am the murderer of King Laius.

JOCASTA:

Did he speak from first-hand knowledge or from hearsay?

OEDIPUS:

He did not speak at all. His lips are pure.
He bribed Tiresias, and that scoundrel spoke.　　　670

JOCASTA:

Then you can rid your mind of any fear
That you are guilty. Listen to me. No mortal
Shares in the gods' foreknowledge. I can give you
Clear proof of that. There came once to King Laius
An oracle—I will not say from Phoebus,
But from his priest—saying it was his fate
That he should be struck down by his own child,
His child and mine. But Laius, as we know,
Was killed by foreign robbers at a place
Where three roads came together. As for the child,　　680
When it was only three days old, its father
Pierced both its ankles, pinned its feet together,
And then gave orders that it be abandoned
On a wild mountainside. So in this case
Phoebus did not fulfill his oracle. The child
Was not its father's murderer, and Laius
Was not the victim of the fate he feared,
Death at his son's hands, although just that fate
Was what the seer predicted. Pay no heed
To prophecies. Whatever may be needful　　　　　690
The god himself can show us easily.

OEDIPUS:

What have you said, Jocasta? What have you said?
The past comes back to me. How terrible!

JOCASTA:

Why do you start so? What has happened to you?

OEDIPUS:

It seemed to me—I thought you said that Laius
Was struck down where three roads came together.

JOCASTA:

I did. That was the story, and still is.

OEDIPUS:

Where was it that this murder was committed?

JOCASTA:

In Phocis, where the road from Thebes divides,
Meeting the roads from Daulia and Delphi.   700

OEDIPUS:

Is this my fate? Is this what the gods decreed?

JOCASTA:

What have I said that has so shaken you?

OEDIPUS:

Do not ask me yet. Tell me about King Laius.
What did he look like? Was he young or old?

JOCASTA:

His build was not unlike yours. He was tall.
His hair was just beginning to turn grey.

OEDIPUS:

I cannot bear the thought that I called down
A curse on my own head unknowingly.

JOCASTA:

What is it, Oedipus? You terrify me!

OEDIPUS:

I dread to think Tiresias had clear eyesight;   710
But tell me one thing more, and I will know.

JOCASTA:

And I too shrink, yet I will answer you.

OEDIPUS:

How did he travel? With a few men only,
Or with his guards and servants, like a prince?

JOCASTA:

There were five of them in all, with one a herald.
They had one carriage in which King Laius rode.

OEDIPUS:

It is too clear, too clear! Who told you this?

JOCASTA:

The only servant who escaped alive.

OEDIPUS:

And is he still here now, still in the palace?

JOCASTA:

No. When he came home and found Laius dead   720
And you the reigning king, he pleaded with me
To send him where the sheep were pasturing,
As far as possible away from Thebes.

And so I sent him. He was a worthy fellow
And, if a slave can, deserved a greater favor.

OEDIPUS:

I hope it is possible to get him quickly.

JOCASTA:

Yes, that is easy. Why do you want to see him?

OEDIPUS:

Because I am afraid, deadly afraid
That I have spoken more than I should have done.

JOCASTA:

He shall come. But Oedipus, have I no right   730
To learn what weighs so heavily on your heart?

OEDIPUS:

You shall learn everything, now that my fears
Have grown so great, for who is dearer to me
Than you, Jocasta? Whom should I speak to sooner,
When I am in such straits? King Polybus
Of Corinth was my father. Meropé,
A Dorian, was my mother. I myself
Was foremost among all the citizens,
Till something happened, strange, but hardly worth
My feeling such resentment. As we sat   740
One day at dinner, a man who had drunk too much
Insulted me by saying I was not
My father's son. In spite of being angry,
I managed to control myself. Next day
I asked my parents, who were both indignant
That he had leveled such a charge against me.
This was a satisfaction, yet the thing
Still rankled, for the rumor grew widespread.
At last I went to Delphi secretly.
Apollo gave no answer to my question   750
But sent me off, anguished and terrified,
With fearful prophecies that I was fated
To be my mother's husband, to bring forth
Children whom men could not endure to see,
And to take my father's life. When I heard this
I turned and fled, hoping to find at length
Some place where I would know of Corinth only
As a far distant land beneath the stars,
Some place where I would never have to see
The infamies of this oracle fulfilled.   760
And as I went on, I approached the spot
At which you tell me Laius met his end.
Now this, Jocasta, is the absolute truth.
When I had come to where the three roads fork,

A herald met me, walking before a carriage,
Drawn by two colts, in which a man was seated,
Just as you said. The old man and the herald
Ordered me off the road with threatening gestures.
Then as the driver pushed me to one side,
I struck him angrily. And seeing this,   770
The old man, as I drew abreast, leaned out
And brought his driver's two-pronged goad down hard
Upon my head. He paid a heavy price
For doing that. With one blow of my staff
I knocked him headlong from his chariot
Flat on his back. Then every man of them
I killed. Now if the blood of Laius flowed
In that old stranger's veins, what mortal man
Could be more wretched, more accursed than I?
I whom no citizen or foreigner   780
May entertain or shelter, I to whom
No one may speak, I, I who must be driven
From every door. No other man has cursed me,
I have brought down this curse upon myself.
The hands that killed him now pollute his bed!
Am I not vile, foul, utterly unclean?
For I must fly and never see again
My people or set foot in my own land,
Or else become the husband of my mother
And put to death my father Polybus,   790
To whom I owe my life and my upbringing.
Men would be right in thinking that such things
Have been inflicted by some cruel fate.
May the gods' high and holy majesty
Forbid that I should see that day. No! No!
Rather than be dishonored by a doom
So dreadful may I vanish from the earth.

CHORUS:

Sir, these are terrible things, but there is hope
Until you have heard what the one witness says.

OEDIPUS:

That is the one remaining hope I have,   800
To wait for the arrival of the shepherd.

JOCASTA:

And when he *has* arrived, what can he do?

OEDIPUS:

He can do this. If his account agrees
With yours, I stand acquitted of this crime.

JOCASTA:

Was what I said of any consequence?

OEDIPUS:

> You said his story was that robbers killed
> King Laius. If he speaks of the same number,
> Then I am not the murderer. One man
> Cannot be several men. But if he says
> One traveler, single-handed, did the deed,   810
> Beyond all doubt the evidence points to me.

JOCASTA:

> I am quite certain that was what he said.
> He cannot change now, for the whole of Thebes
> Heard it, not I alone. In any case,
> Even supposing that his story *should*
> Be somewhat different, he can never make
> Laius's death fulfill the oracle.
> Phoebus said plainly Laius was to die
> At my son's hands. However, that poor child
> Certainly did not kill him, for it died   820
> Before its father. I would not waste my time
> In giving any thought to prophecy.

OEDIPUS:

> Yes, you are right. And yet have someone sent
> To bring the shepherd here. Make sure of this.

JOCASTA:

> I will, at once. Come, Oedipus, come in.
> I will do nothing that you disapprove of.
>
> > *Exeunt* OEDIPUS *and* JOCASTA

CHORUS:

> May piety and reverence mark my actions;
>   May every thought be pure through all my days.
> May those great laws whose dwelling is in heaven
>   Approve my conduct with their crown of praise: 830
> Offspring of skies that overarch Olympus,
>   Laws from the loins of no mere mortal sprung,
> Unslumbering, unfailing, unforgetting,
>   Filled with a godhead that is ever young.
>
> Pride breeds the tyrant. Insolent presumption,
>   Big with delusive wealth and false renown,
> Once it has mounted to the highest rampart
>   Is headlong hurled in utter ruin down.
> But pour out all thy blessings, Lord Apollo,
>   Thou who alone hast made and kept us great,   840
> On all whose sole ambition is unselfish,
>   Who spend themselves in service to the state.

Let that man be accurséd who is proud,
In act unscrupulous, in thinking base,
   Whose knees in reverence have never bowed,
In whose hard heart justice can find no place,
   Whose hands profane life's holiest mysteries,
How can he hope to shield himself for long
   From the gods' arrows that will pierce him through?
If evil triumphs in such ways as these,   850
   Why should we seek, in choric dance and song,
To give the gods the praise that is their due?

   I cannot go in full faith as of old,
To sacred Delphi or Olympian vale,
   Unless men see that what has been foretold
Has come to pass, that omens never fail.
   All-ruling Zeus, if thou art King indeed,
Put forth thy majesty, make good thy word,
   Faith in these fading oracles restore!
To priest and prophet men pay little heed;   860
   Hymns to Apollo are no longer heard;
And all religion soon will be no more.

Enter JOCASTA

JOCASTA:
   Elders of Thebes, I thought that I should visit
   The altars of the gods to offer up
   These wreaths I carry and these gifts of incense.
   The King is overanxious, overtroubled.
   He is no longer calm enough to judge
   The present by the lessons of the past,
   But trembles before anyone who brings
   An evil prophecy. I cannot help him.   870
   Therefore, since thou art nearest, bright Apollo,
   I bring these offerings to thee. O, hear me!
   Deliver us from this defiling curse.
   His fear infects us all, as if we were
   Sailors who saw their pilot terrified.

Enter MESSENGER

MESSENGER:
   Sirs, I have come to find King Oedipus.
   Where is his palace, can you tell me that?
   Or better yet, where is the King himself?
CHORUS:
   Stranger, the King is there, within his palace.
   This is the Queen, the mother of his children.   880

MESSENGER:

> May all the gods be good to you and yours!
> Madam, you are a lady richly blessed.

JOCASTA:

> And may the gods requite your courtesy.
> But what request or message do you bring us?

MESSENGER:

> Good tidings for your husband and your household.

JOCASTA:

> What is your news? What country do you come from?

MESSENGER:

> From Corinth. And the news I bring will surely
> Give you great pleasure—and perhaps some pain.

JOCASTA:

> What message can be good and bad at once?

MESSENGER:

> The citizens of Corinth, it is said,   890
> Have chosen Oedipus to be their King.

JOCASTA:

> What do you mean? Their King is Polybus.

MESSENGER:

> No, madam. Polybus is dead and buried.

JOCASTA:

> What! Dead! The father of King Oedipus?

MESSENGER:

> If I speak falsely, let me die myself.

JOCASTA (*to* ATTENDANT):

> Go find the King and tell him this. Be quick!
> What does an oracle amount to now?
> This is the man whom Oedipus all these years
> Has feared and shunned to keep from killing him,
> And now we find he dies a natural death!   900

Enter OEDIPUS

OEDIPUS:

> My dear Jocasta, why have you sent for me?

JOCASTA:

> Listen to this man's message, and then tell me
> What faith you have in sacred oracles.

OEDIPUS:

> Where does he come from? What has he to say?

JOCASTA:

> He comes from Corinth and has this to say:
> The King, your father, Polybus is dead.

OEDIPUS (*to* MESSENGER):

> My father! Tell me that again yourself.

MESSENGER:

    I will say first what you first want to know.
    You may be certain he is dead and gone .

OEDIPUS:

    How did he die? By violence or sickness?   910

MESSENGER:

    The scales of life tip easily for the old.

OEDIPUS:

    That is to say he died of some disease.

MESSENGER:

    Yes, of disease, and merely of old age.

OEDIPUS:

    Hear that, Jocasta! Why should anyone
    Give heed to oracles from the Pythian shrine,
    Or to the birds that shriek above our heads?
    They prophesied that I must kill my father.
    But he is dead; the earth has covered him.
    And I am here, I who have never raised
    My hand against him—unless he died of grief,   920
    Longing to see me. Then I might be said
    To have caused his death. But as they stand, at least,
    The oracles have been swept away like rubbish.
    They are with Polybus in Hades, dead.

JOCASTA:

    Long ago, Oedipus, I told you that.

OEDIPUS:

    You did, but I was blinded by my terror.

JOCASTA:

    Now you need take these things to heart no longer.

OEDIPUS:

    But there is still my mother's bed to fear.

JOCASTA:

    Why should you be afraid? Chance rules our lives,
    And no one can foresee the future, no one.   930
    We live best when we live without a purpose
    From one day to the next. Forget your fear
    Of marrying your mother. That has happened
    To many men before this in their dreams.
    We find existence most endurable
    When such things are neglected and forgotten.

OEDIPUS:

    That would be true, Jocasta, if my mother
    Were not alive; but now your eloquence
    Is not enough to give me reassurance.

JOCASTA:

    And yet your father's death is a great comfort.   940

OEDIPUS:

    Yes, but I cannot rest while she is living.

MESSENGER:

    Sir, will you tell me who it is you fear?

OEDIPUS:

    Queen Meropé, the wife of Polybus.

MESSENGER:

    What is so terrible about the Queen?

OEDIPUS:

    A dreadful prophecy the gods have sent us.

MESSENGER:

    Are you forbidden to speak of it, or not?

OEDIPUS:

    It may be told. The Lord Apollo said
    That I was doomed to marry my own mother,
    And shed my father's blood with my own hands.
    And so for years I have stayed away from Corinth,   950
    My native land—a fortunate thing for me,
    Though it is very sweet to see one's parents.

MESSENGER:

    Was that the reason you have lived in exile?

OEDIPUS:

    Yes, for I feared my mother and my father.

MESSENGER:

    Then since my journey was to wish you well,
    Let me release you from your fear at once.

OEDIPUS:

    That would deserve my deepest gratitude.

MESSENGER:

    Sir, I *did* come here with the hope of earning
    Some recompense when you had gotten home.

OEDIPUS:

    No. I will never again go near my home.   960

MESSENGER:

    O son, son! You know nothing. That is clear—

OEDIPUS:

    What do you mean, old friend? Tell me, I beg you.

MESSENGER:

    If that is why you dare not come to Corinth.

OEDIPUS:

    I fear Apollo's word would be fulfilled.

MESSENGER:

    That you would be polluted through your parents?

OEDIPUS:

    Yes, yes! My life is haunted by that horror.

MESSENGER:

    You have no reason to be horrified.

OEDIPUS:

I have no reason! Why? They are my parents.

MESSENGER:

No. You are not the son of Polybus.

OEDIPUS:

What did you say? Polybus not my father?   970

MESSENGER:

He was as much your father as I am.

OEDIPUS:

How can that be—my father like a stranger?

MESSENGER:

But he was *not* your father, nor am I.

OEDIPUS:

If that is so, why was I called his son?

MESSENGER:

Because he took you as a gift, from me.

OEDIPUS:

Yet even so, he loved me like a father?

MESSENGER:

Yes, for he had no children of his own.

OEDIPUS:

And when you gave me, had you bought or found me?

MESSENGER:

I found you in the glens of Mount Cithaeron.

OEDIPUS:

What could have brought you to a place like that?   980

MESSENGER:

The flocks of sheep that I was tending there.

OEDIPUS:

You went from place to place, hunting for work?

MESSENGER:

I did, my son. And yet I saved your life.

OEDIPUS:

How? Was I suffering when you took me up?

MESSENGER:

Your ankles are the proof of what you suffered.

OEDIPUS:

That misery! Why do you speak of that?

MESSENGER:

Your feet were pinned together, and I freed them.

OEDIPUS:

Yes. From my cradle I have borne those scars.

MESSENGER:

They are the reason for your present name.

OEDIPUS:

Who did it? Speak! My mother, or my father?   990

69

MESSENGER:

Only the man who gave you to me knows.

OEDIPUS:

Then you yourself did not discover me.

MESSENGER:

No. A man put you in my arms, some shepherd.

OEDIPUS:

Do you know who he was? Can you describe him?

MESSENGER:

He was, I think, one of the slaves of Laius.

OEDIPUS:

The Laius who was once the King of Thebes?

MESSENGER:

Yes, that is right. King Laius was his master.

OEDIPUS:

How could I see him? Is he still alive?

MESSENGER:

One of his fellow Thebans would know that.

OEDIPUS:

Does anyone here know who this shepherd is?   1000
Has anyone ever seen him in the city
Or in the fields? Tell me. Now is the time
To solve this mystery once and for all.

CHORUS:

Sir, I believe the shepherd whom he means
Is the same man you have already sent for.
The Queen, perhaps, knows most about the matter.

OEDIPUS:

Do you, Jocasta? You know the man we summoned.
Is he the man this messenger spoke about?

JOCASTA:

Why do you care? What difference can it make?
To ask is a waste of time, a waste of time!   1010

OEDIPUS:

I cannot let these clues slip from my hands.
I must track down the secret of my birth.

JOCASTA:

Oedipus, Oedipus! By all the gods,
If you set any value on your life,
Give up this search! I have endured enough.

OEDIPUS:

Do not be frightened. Even if my mother
Should prove to be a slave, and born of slaves,
This would not touch the honor of your name.

JOCASTA:

Listen, I beg you! Listen! Do not do this!

OEDIPUS:
I cannot fail to bring the truth to light.   1020
JOCASTA:
I know my way is best for you, I know it!
OEDIPUS:
I know your best way is unbearable.
JOCASTA:
May you be saved from learning who you are!
OEDIPUS:
Go, someone. Bring the shepherd. As for her,
Let her take comfort in her noble birth.
JOCASTA:
You are lost! Lost! That is all I can call you now!
That is all I will ever call you, ever again!

Exit JOCASTA

CHORUS:
What wild grief, sir, has driven the Queen away?
Evil, I fear, will follow from her silence,
A storm of sorrow that will break upon us.   1030
OEDIPUS:
Then let it break upon us. I must learn
My parentage, whatever it may be.
The Queen is proud, far prouder than most women,
And feels herself dishonored by my baseness.
But I shall not be shamed. I hold myself
The child of Fortune, giver of all good.
She brought me forth. And as I lived my life,
The months, my brothers, watched the ebb and flow
Of my well-being. Never could I prove
False to a lineage like that, or fail   1040
To bring to light the secret of my birth.
CHORUS:
May Phoebus grant that I prove a true prophet!
    My heart foreknows what the future will bring:
At tomorrow's full moon we shall gather, in chorus
    To hail Cithaeron, to dance and sing
In praise of the mountain by Oedipus honored,
    Theban nurse of our Theban King.

What long-lived nymph was the mother who bore you?
    What god whom the joys of the hills invite
Was the god who begot you? Pan? or Apollo?   1050
    Or Hermes, Lord of Cylené's height?
Or on Helicon's slope did an oread place you
    In Bacchus's arms for his new delight?

OEDIPUS:

Elders, I think I see the shepherd coming
Whom we have sent for. Since I never met him,
I am not sure, yet he seems old enough,
And my own slaves are the men bringing him.
But you, perhaps, know more of this than I,
If any of you have seen the man before.

CHORUS:

Yes, it is he. I know him, the King's shepherd,   1060
As true a slave as Laius ever had.

Enter SHEPHERD

OEDIPUS:

I start with you, Corinthian. Is this man
The one you spoke of?   MESS.: Sir, he stands before you.

OEDIPUS:

Now you, old man. Come, look me in the face.
Answer my questions. You were the slave of Laius?

SHEPHERD:

Yes, but not bought. I grew up in his household.

OEDIPUS:

What was the work that you were given to do?

SHEPHERD:

Sheep-herding. I have always been a shepherd.

OEDIPUS:

Where was it that you took your sheep to pasture?

SHEPHERD:

On Mount Cithaeron, or the fields near by.   1070

OEDIPUS:

Do you remember seeing this man there?

SHEPHERD:

What was he doing? What man do you mean?

OEDIPUS:

That man beside you. Have you ever met him?

SHEPHERD:

No, I think not. I cannot recollect him.

MESSENGER:

Sir, I am not surprised, but I am sure
That I can make the past come back to him.
He cannot have forgotten the long summers
We grazed our sheep together by Cithaeron,
He with two flocks, and I with one—three years,
From spring to autumn. Then, for the winter months,   1080
I used to drive my sheep to their own fold,
And he drove his back to the fold of Laius.
Is that right? Did it happen as I said?

SHEPHERD:

Yes, you are right, but it was long ago.

MESSENGER:

Well then, do you remember you once gave me
An infant boy to bring up as my own?

SHEPHERD:

What do you mean? Why do you ask me that?

MESSENGER:

Because the child you gave me stands before you.

SHEPHERD:

Will you be quiet? Curse you! Will you be quiet?

OEDIPUS (*to* SHEPHERD):

You there! You have no reason to be angry.   1090
You are far more to blame in this than he.

SHEPHERD:

What have I done, my Lord? What have I done?

OEDIPUS:

You have not answered. He asked about the boy.

SHEPHERD:

Sir, he knows nothing, nothing at all about it.

OEDIPUS:

And you say nothing. We must make you speak.

SHEPHERD:

My Lord, I am an old man! Do not hurt me!

OEDIPUS (*to* GUARDS):

One of you tie his hands behind his back.

SHEPHERD:

Why do you want to know these fearful things?

OEDIPUS:

Did you, or did you not, give him that child?

SHEPHERD:

I did. I wish that I had died instead.   1100

OEDIPUS:

You will die now, unless you tell the truth.

SHEPHERD:

And if I speak, I will be worse than dead.

OEDIPUS:

You seem to be determined to delay.

SHEPHERD:

No. No! I told you that I had the child.

OEDIPUS:

Where did it come from? Was it yours or not?

SHEPHERD:

No, it was not mine. Someone gave it to me.

OEDIPUS:

Some citizen of Thebes? Who was it? Who?

SHEPHERD:

    Oh! Do not ask me that! Not that, my Lord!

OEDIPUS:

    If I must ask once more, you are a dead man.

SHEPHERD:

    The child came from the household of King Laius.   1110

OEDIPUS:

    Was it a slave's child? Or of royal blood?

SHEPHERD:

    I stand on the very brink of speaking horrors.

OEDIPUS:

    And I of hearing horrors—but I must.

SHEPHERD:

    Then hear. The child was said to be the King's.
    You can best learn about this from the Queen.

OEDIPUS:

    The Queen! She gave it to you?   SHEP.: Yes, my Lord.

OEDIPUS:

    Why did she do that?   SHEP.: So that I should kill it.

OEDIPUS:

    Her own child?   SHEP.: Yes, she feared the oracles.

OEDIPUS:

    What oracles?   SHEP.: That it must kill its father.

OEDIPUS:

    Then why did you give it up to this old man?   1120

SHEPHERD:

    I pitied the poor child. I thought the man
    Would take it with him back to his own country.
    He saved its life only to have it come
    At last to this. If you should be the man
    He says you are, you were born miserable.

OEDIPUS:

    All true! All, all made clear! Let me no longer
    Look on the light of day. I am known now
    For what I am—I, cursed in being born,
    Cursed in my marriage, cursed in the blood I shed.

                           Exit OEDIPUS

CHORUS:

    Men are of little worth. Their brief lives last   1130
        A single day.
    They cannot hold elusive pleasure fast;
        It melts away.
    All laurels wither; all illusions fade;
    Hopes have been phantoms, shade on air-built shade,
        Since time began.

Your fate, O King, your fate makes manifest
Life's wretchedness. We can call no one blessed,
    No, not one man.

Victorious, unerring, to their mark   1140
    Your arrows flew.
The Sphinx with her curved claws, her riddle dark,
    Your wisdom slew.
By this encounter you preserved us all,
Guarding the land from death's approach, our tall,
    Unshaken tower.
From that time, Oedipus, we held you dear,
Great King of our great Thebes, without a peer
    In place and power.

But now what sadder story could be told?   1150
    A life of triumph utterly undone!
What fate could be more grievous to behold?
    Father and son
Both found a sheltering port, a place of rest,
    On the same breast.
Father and son both harvested the yield
    Of the same bounteous field.
How could that earth endure such dreadful wrong
    And hold its peace so long?

All-seeing time condemned your marriage lot;   1160
    In ways you least expected bared its shame—
Union wherein begetter and begot
    Were both the same.
This loud lament, these tears that well and flow,
    This bitter woe
Are for the day you rescued us, O King,
    From our great suffering;
For the new life and happiness you gave
    You drag down to the grave.

Enter SECOND MESSENGER

SECOND MESSENGER:
    Most honored elders, princes of the land,   1170
    If you are true-born Thebans and still love
    The house of Labdacus, then what a burden
    Of sorrow you must bear, what fearful things
    You must now hear and see! There is no river—
    No, not the stream of Ister or of Phasis—
    That could wash clean this house from the pollution

It hides within it or will soon bring forth:
Horrible deeds not done in ignorance,
But done deliberately. The cruelest evils
Are those that we embrace with open eyes.   1180

CHORUS:

Those we already know of are enough
To claim our tears. What more have you to tell?

SECOND MESSENGER:

It may be briefly told. The Queen is dead.

CHORUS:

Poor woman! oh, poor woman! How? What happened?

SECOND MESSENGER:

She killed herself. You have been spared the worst,
Not being witnesses. Yet you shall learn
What her fate was, so far as I remember.
When she came in, almost beside herself,
Clutching her hair with both her hands, she rushed
Straight to her bedroom and slammed shut the doors   1190
Behind her, screaming the name of Laius—
Laius long dead, but not her memory
Of their own child, the son who killed his father,
The son by whom his mother had more children.
She cursed the bed in which she had conceived
Husband by husband, children by her child,
A dreadful double bond. Beyond this much
I do not know the manner of her death,
For with a great cry Oedipus burst in,
Preventing us from following her fate   1200
To its dark end. On him our gaze was fixed,
As in a frenzy he ran to and fro,
Calling: 'Give me a sword! Give me a sword!
Where is that wife who is no wife, that mother,
That soil where I was sower and was sown?'
And as he raved, those of us there did nothing,
Some more than mortal power directed him.
With a wild shriek, as though he had some sign,
He hurled himself against the double doors,
Forcing the bars out of their loosened sockets,   1210
And broke into his room. There was the Queen,
Hanged in a noose, still swinging back and forth.
When he saw this, the King cried out in anguish,
Untied the knotted cord in which she swung,
And laid the wretched woman on the ground.
What happened then was terrible to see.
He tore the golden brooches from her robe,
Lifted them up as high as he could reach,

And drove them with all his strength into his eyes,
Shrieking, 'No more, no more shall my eyes see   1220
The horrors of my life—what I have done,
What I have suffered. They have looked too long
On those whom they ought never to have seen.
They never knew those whom I longed to see.
Blind, blind! Let them be blind!' With these wild words
He stabbed and stabbed his eyes. At every blow,
The dark blood dyed his beard, not sluggish drops,
But a great torrent like a shower of hail.
A two-fold punishment of two-fold sin
Broke on the heads of husband and of wife.   1230
Their happiness was once true happiness,
But now disgrace has come upon them, death,
Sorrow, and ruin, every earthly ill
That can be named. Not one have they escaped.

CHORUS:
Is he still suffering? Has he found relief?

SECOND MESSENGER:
He calls for someone to unbar the doors
And show him to all Thebes, his father's killer,
His mother's—no, I cannot say the word;
It is unholy, horrible. He intends
To leave the country, for his staying here
Would bring down his own curse upon his house.   1240
He has no guide and no strength of his own.
His pain is unendurable. This too
You will see. They are drawing back the bars.
The sight is loathsome and yet pitiful.

Enter OEDIPUS

CHORUS:
Hideous, hideous! I have seen nothing so dreadful,
Ever before!
I can look no more.
Oedipus, Oedipus! What madness has come upon you?
What malignant fate
Has leaped with its full weight,   1250
Has struck you down with an irresistible fury,
And born you off as its prey?
Poor wretch! There is much that I yearn
To ask of you, much I would learn;
But I cannot. The sight of you fills me with horror!
I shudder and turn away.

OEDIPUS:

    Oh, Oh! What pain! I cannot rest in my anguish!
       Where am I? Where?
    Where are my words? They die away as I speak them,
       Into thin air.   1260
       What is my fate to be?

CHORUS: A fate too fearful for men to hear of, for men to see.

OEDIPUS: Lost! Overwhelmed by the rush of unspeakable darkness!
       It smothers me in its cloud.
       The pain of my eyes is piercing.
    The thought of my sins, the horrors that I have committed,
       Racks me without relief.

CHORUS: No wonder you suffer, Oedipus, no wonder you cry aloud
       Under your double burden of pain and grief.

OEDIPUS: My friend, my friend! How steadfast you are, how ready 1270
       To help me in my great need!
       I feel your presence beside me.
    Blind as I am, I know your voice in the blackness
       Of my long-lasting night.

CHORUS: How could you put out your eyes, still another infamous deed?
       What god, what demon, induced you to quench their light?

OEDIPUS: It was Apollo, my friends, who brought me low,
    Apollo who crushed me beneath this unbearable burden;
       But it was my hand, mine, that struck the blow.
    Why should I see? What sight could have given me pleasure?

CHORUS: These things are as you say.

OEDIPUS: What is there now to love? What greeting can cheer me?
       Lead me away,
    Quickly, quickly! O lead me out of the country
       To a distant land! I am beyond redemption
    Accursed, beyond hope lost, the one man living
       Whom all the gods most hate.

CHORUS: Would we had never heard of your existence,
       Your fruitless wisdom and your wretched fate.

OEDIPUS: My curses be upon him, whoever freed   1290
    My feet from the cruel fetters, there on the mountain,
       Who restored me from death to life, a thankless deed.
    My death would have saved my friends and me from anguish.

CHORUS: I too would have had it so.
OEDIPUS: Then would I never have been my father's killer.
        Now all men know
    That I am the infamous son who defiled his mother,
      That I shared the bed of the father who gave me being.
    And if there is sorrow beyond any mortal sorrow,
      I have brought it upon my head.   1300
CHORUS: I cannot say that you have acted wisely.
      Alive and blind? You would be better dead.

OEDIPUS:
    Give me no more advice, and do not tell me
    That I was wrong. What I have done is best.
    For if I still had eyesight when I went
    Down to the underworld, how could I bear
    To see my father and my wretched mother?
    After the terrible wrong I did them both,
    It would not have been punishment enough
    If I had hanged myself. Or do you think   1310
    That I could find enjoyment in the sight
    Of children born as mine were born? No! No!
    Nor in the sight of Thebes with its towered walls
    And sacred statues of the gods. For I—
    Who is so wretched?—I, the foremost Theban,
    Cut myself off from this by my own edict
    That ordered everyone to shun the man
    Polluting us, the man the gods have shown
    To be accursed, and of the house of Laius.
    Once I laid bare my shame, could I endure   1320
    To look my fellow-citizens in the face?
    Never! Never! If I had found some way
    Of choking off the fountain of my hearing,
    I would have made a prison of my body,
    Sightless and soundless. It would be sweet to live
    Beyond the reach of sorrow. Oh, Cithaeron!
    Why did you give me shelter rather than slay me
    As soon as I was given to you? Then
    No one would ever have heard of my begetting.
    Polybus, Corinth, and the ancient house   1330
    I thought my forebears'! You reared me as a child.
    My fair appearance covered foul corruption,
    I am impure, born of impurity.
    Oh, narrow crossroad where the three paths meet!
    Secluded valley hidden in the forest,

You that drank up my blood, my father's blood
Shed by my hands, do you remember all
I did for you to see? Do you remember
What else I did when I came here to Thebes?
Oh marriage rites! By which I was begotten,   1340
You then brought forth children by your own child,
Creating foulest blood-relationship:
An interchange of fathers, brothers, sons,
Brides, wives, and mothers—the most monstrous shame
Man can be guilty of. I should not speak
Of what should not be done. By all the gods,
Hide me, I beg you, hide me quickly somewhere
Far, far away. Put me to death or throw me
Into the sea, out of your sight forever.
Come to me, friends, pity my wretchedness.   1350
Let your hands touch me. Hear me. Do not fear,
My curse can rest on no one but myself.

CHORUS:

Creon is coming. He is the one to act
On your requests, or to help you with advice.
He takes your place as our sole guardian.

OEDIPUS:

Creon! What shall I say? I cannot hope
That he will trust me now, when my past hatred
Has proved to be so utterly mistaken.

Enter CREON

CREON:

I have not come to mock you, Oedipus,
Or to reproach you for any evil-doing.   1360
(*to* ATTENDANTS) You there. If you have lost all your respect
For men, revere at least the Lord Apollo,
Whose flame supports all life. Do not display
So nakedly pollution such as this,
Evil that neither earth nor holy rain
Nor light of day can welcome. Take him in,
Take him in, quickly. Piety demands
That only kinsmen share a kinsman's woe.

OEDIPUS:

Creon, since you have proved my fears were groundless,
Since you have shown such magnanimity   1370
To one so vile as I, grant my petition.
I ask you not for my sake but your own.

CREON:
> What is it that you beg so urgently?

OEDIPUS:
> Drive me away at once. Drive me far off.
> Let me not hear a human voice again.

CREON:
> I have delayed only because I wished
> To have the god reveal to me my duty.

OEDIPUS:
> But his command was certain: put to death
> The unholy parricide. And I am he.

CREON:
> True. But as things are now, it would be better 1380
> To find out clearly what we ought to do.

OEDIPUS:
> An oracle for a man so miserable?

CREON:
> Yes. Even you will now believe the god.

OEDIPUS:
> I will. Creon, I charge you with this duty.
> Accept it, I entreat you. Give to her
> Who lies within such burial as you wish,
> For she belongs to you. You will perform
> The proper obsequies. But as for me,
> Let not my presence doom my father's city,
> But send me to the hills, to Mount Cithaeron, 1390
> *My* mountain, which my mother and my father
> Chose for my grave. So will I die at last
> By the decree of those who sought to slay me.
> And yet I know I will not die from sickness
> Or anything else. I was preserved from death
> To meet some awful, some mysterious end.
> My own fate does not matter, only my children's.
> Creon, my sons need give you no concern,
> For they are men, and can find anywhere
> A livelihood. But Creon, my two girls! 1400
> How lost, how pitiable! They always ate
> Their daily bread with me, at my own table,
> And had their share of everything I touched.
> Take care of them! O Creon, take care of them!
> And one thing more—if I could only touch them
> And with them weep. O prince, prince, grant me this!
> Grant it, O noble Creon! If I touched them,
> I could believe I saw them once again.

Enter ISMENE *and* ANTIGONE

What! Do I hear my daughters? Hear them sobbing?
Has Creon had pity on me? Has he sent them,   1410
My children, my two darlings? Is it true?

CREON:

Yes. I have had them brought. I knew how much
You used to love them, how you love them still.

OEDIPUS:

May the gods bless you, Creon, for this kindness;
And may they guard you better on your journey
Than they have guarded me. Children, where are you?
Come to your brother's hands, the hands that made
Your father's clear eyes into what these are—
Your father, who saw nothing and knew nothing,
Begetting you where he had been conceived.   1420
I cannot see you, but I weep for you,
Weep for the bitter lives that you must lead
Henceforward. Never, never will you go
To an assembly with the citizens,
Or to a festival, and take your part.
You will turn back in tears. And when you come
To the full bloom of womanhood, what man
Will run the risk of bringing on himself
Your shame, my daughters, and your children's shame?
Is there one evil, one, that is not ours?   1430
'Your father killed his father; he begot
Children of his own mother; she who bore you
Bore him as well.' These are the taunts, the insults
That you will hear. Who, then, will marry you?
No one, my children. Clearly it is your fate
To waste away in barren maidenhood.
Creon, Creon, their blood flows in your veins.
You are the only father left to them;
They have lost both their parents. Do not let them
Wander away, unmarried, destitute,   1440
As miserable as I. Have pity on them,
So young, so utterly forlorn, so helpless
Except for you. You are kind-hearted. Touch me
To tell me that I have your promise. Children,
There is so much, so much that I would say,
If you were old enough to understand it,
But now I only teach you this one prayer:
May I be given a place in which to live,
And may my life be happier than my father's.

CREON:

    Come, come with us. Have done with further woe.   1450

OE.:   Obedience is hard. CR.: No good in life endures beyond
        its season.

OE.:   Do you know why I yield? CR.: When I have heard your
        reason I will know.

OE.:   You are to banish me. CR.: The gods alone can grant you
        that entreaty.

OE.:   I am hated by the gods. CR.: Then their response to you
        will not be slow.

OE.:   So you consent to this? CR.: I say no more than I have
        said already.

OE.:   Come, then, lead me away. CR.: Not with your children.
        You must let them go.

OE.:   Creon, not that, not that! CR.: You must be patient.
        Nothing can restore
    Your old dominion. You are King no more.

Exeunt CREON, OEDIPUS, ISMENE, *and* ANTIGONE

CHORUS:

    Behold him, Thebans: Oedipus, great and wise,
    Who solved the famous riddle. This is he   1460
      Whom all men gazed upon with envious eyes,
    Who now is struggling in a stormy sea,
      Crushed by the billows of his bitter woes.
    Look to the end of mortal life. In vain
      We say a man is happy, till he goes
    Beyond life's final border, free from pain.

Oedipus at Colonus

CHARACTERS IN THE PLAY

OEDIPUS, *former King of Thebes*

ANTIGONE
ISMENE } *his daughters*

POLYNEICES, *his son*

THESEUS, *King of Athens*

CREON, *King of Thebes, brother of* JOCASTA, *the wife and mother of* OEDIPUS

COUNTRYMAN, *a native of Colonus*

MESSENGER

CHORUS, *elders of Colonus*

ATTENDANTS

OEDIPUS AT COLONUS

SCENE: *The countryside. In the background there is a thick grove of trees, on the edge of which stands a large rock.*

Enter OEDIPUS *in rags, guided by* ANTIGONE

OEDIPUS:

    Antigone, where is your blind old father?
    Still in the countryside, or near some city?
    Who is it that will give his grudging gifts,
    His scanty hospitality, today
    To wandering Oedipus? I ask for little.
    Though I get less than little, it is enough;
    For hardship and the years that have been my lot,
    The long years, and nobility of mind
    Have taught me patience. Daughter, if you can see
    A place of rest, either unhallowed ground   10
    Or sacred grove, help me to find a seat.
    For we must ask some citizen where we are,
    And we must do whatever we are bidden.

ANTIGONE:

    Father, the walls and towers that I see
    Guarding the city seem to be far away,
    And this spot where we stand is surely sacred.
    For laurels, vines, and olives grow profusely,
    And deep within, a throng of nightingales
    Pour out their eloquence. So rest here, Father.
    There is a natural seat here in the rock.   20
    You have come a long, long way, and you are old.

OEDIPUS:

    Then seat the blind man and take care of him.

ANTIGONE:

    If time can teach me, I have learned that lesson.

OEDIPUS:

    Where have we come to, Daughter? Can you tell me?

ANTIGONE:

    Athens I know well, but this place is strange.

OEDIPUS:

    You say what everyone we met has said.

ANTIGONE:

What shall I do? Go find out where we are?

OEDIPUS:

Yes, if you think there are people living here.

ANTIGONE:

Surely there are. And yet I need not go,
For I see someone now, not far away.   30

OEDIPUS:

Coming in this direction? Coming near?

ANTIGONE:

He has come close to us already. Say
Whatever you think is best, for he is here.

Enter COUNTRYMAN

OEDIPUS:

Stranger, this girl has eyes for both of us.
Hearing from her of your most timely coming
To give us aid in our perplexity—

COUNTRYMAN:

Speak not a word more. Let your story wait
Till you have come from that forbidden ground.

OEDIPUS:

Forbidden ground? To which god is it sacred?

COUNTRYMAN:

Holy and unapproachable, it belongs   40
To the terrible daughters of Darkness and of Earth.

OEDIPUS:

Whose awful name am I to hear and pray to?

COUNTRYMAN:

We call them the Eumenides, the all-seeing,
The Goddesses Benignant. But elsewhere
Men do them honor under other names.

OEDIPUS:

May they receive their suppliant graciously!
This is the seat that I will never leave.

COUNTRYMAN:

What do you mean? OE.: I have been given a sign.

COUNTRYMAN:

I dare not act myself and drive you out.
The citizens must sanction what I do.   50

OEDIPUS:

For the love of all the gods, sir, I entreat you
Not to refuse a wanderer such as I,
Not to refuse to tell me what I ask.

COUNTRYMAN:

Speak. You will find that I shall not refuse you.

OEDIPUS:

Then what is the name of the place that we have entered?

COUNTRYMAN:

You shall hear everything that I can tell you.
The whole vicinity is hallowed ground,
Held by august Poseidon and the Titan,
Prometheus the fire-bringing god. The spot
On which you stand is the mainstay of Athens,   60
Known as the Brazen Threshold of the land.
The neighboring fields claim for their founding lord
Colonus the horseman, and the people bear
His name as well. Now you may understand
This is a country honored not in legend
But in the hearts of its inhabitants.

OEDIPUS:

Then it is true that men are living here?

COUNTRYMAN:

It is. They are the namesakes of the hero.

OEDIPUS:

Have they a king? Or do they rule themselves?

COUNTRYMAN:

The city's king is the ruler of this region.   70

OEDIPUS:

Who is this man, sovereign in word and act?

COUNTRYMAN:

Theseus, the son of Aegeus, king before him.

OEDIPUS:

And could a messenger be sent to him?

COUNTRYMAN:

What should the man say? Urge the King to come?

OEDIPUS:

By a small service the King will profit greatly.

COUNTRYMAN:

How, in your blindness, can you bring him profit?

OEDIPUS:

In every word I utter there shall be vision.

COUNTRYMAN:

Sir, let me teach you how to save yourself,
For it appears to me your birth is noble
In spite of your ill-fortune. Stay where you are,   80
Where you first showed yourself, until I tell
The people of Colonus, not of Athens,
All that has happened here. They will decide
Whether you are to leave or to remain.

Exit COUNTRYMAN

OEDIPUS:

Tell me, Antigone, is the stranger gone?

ANTIGONE:

> Yes, he is gone. Say what you will in peace,
> You may be sure that only I am near.

OEDIPUS:

> O queens, O goddesses, terrible to behold!
> Since my first refuge was this shrine of yours,
> Close not your hearts to Phoebus and to me.　　　　90
> When by his oracle the god proclaimed
> The many evils that have come upon me,
> This too he promised: that after many years
> I should at length attain my final rest,
> Rest from my sorrow and my weariness,
> When in some land that made a stranger welcome
> I found the shrine of the Dread Goddesses;
> And that my presence in the land would bring
> A blessing upon those who sheltered me,
> But upon those who banished me a curse.　　　　100
> The god forewarned that signs of this would come,
> Perhaps in earthquake, thunder, or the flash
> Of Zeus's lightning. Now it is clear to me
> That in my journey some sure prompting led me
> On to this grove—your prompting, goddesses.
> How else could I have come upon you here,
> When first I set my foot within the land,
> I who live sparely, you whom wine delights not?
> How else could I have found this holy seat
> Not hewn by mortal hands? Then, goddesses,　　　　110
> According to the prophecy of Apollo,
> Grant that I may forthwith attain my goal,
> The close of my life's course, unless I seem
> Unworthy of such grace, I who have been
> Slave to the heaviest ills that men endure.
> Hear me, kind daughters of primeval Darkness!
> Hear me, O city held in highest honor:
> Athens, the city of the mighty Pallas!
> Have pity on this poor phantom, for in truth
> I am no more the Oedipus of old.　　　　120

ANTIGONE:

> Hush, Father, hush. Some old men, white with years,
> Have come to seek you in your sanctuary.

OEDIPUS:

> I will say nothing. Hide me among the trees
> Till I discover what those men will say,
> For we are safe only when we have knowledge.

> *Exeunt. Enter the* CHORUS

CHORUS:
>> Search for him! Search! Beware!
> Where is he? Where has he fled?
>> Where is he hidden, where?
> This man without shame, without dread.
> Surely he must be a stranger—not one of our race.   130
>> Wandering here from afar has the old man come.
> Who else would enter the sacred, untrodden place?
>> All-powerful maidens, whose name we tremble to say!
>> We pass your shrine turning our eyes away,
> Breathing our words of devotion with lips that are dumb.
>> But now we have learned that an impious man is here,
> Whose heart is untouched with awe in this holy spot.
>> Closely I search, for I know he is hidden near,
>>> Yet I find him not.

OEDIPUS:
>> Then search for him no longer. I am he,   140
> A man whose ears must take the place of eyes.

CHORUS: Dreadful he is to hear! Dreadful to see!

OEDIPUS: The gods, believe me, I do not despise.

CHORUS: Heaven preserve us! Who can this old man be?

OEDIPUS: Not one whose fortune you should greatly prize.
>> Another leads me, creeping helplessly,
> And all my strength on a frail reed relies.

CHORUS:
>> Blind? Blind from your birth?
> A stranger stricken in years,
>> A wanderer over the earth!   150
> How bitter your life appears!
> How heavy the burden of fate that has bowed your head!
>> I would save you from adding this curse to the ills you bear.
> Hear me! Give heed! Rashly, profanely you tread
>> The inviolate grove where water and honey flow
> In libations together. Too far, too far you go!
> Can you hear us, old man? Do our voices reach you there?
>> Come back to us here, where speech is allowed to all.
> Then you may say what you will; but speak not a word
>> Until you have left that ground where no foot may fall,
>>> No voice may be heard.

OEDIPUS:
>> What shall we do, Antigone? What is best?

ANTIGONE: Follow their custom, Father. It is clear
>> We should submit and do what they request.

OEDIPUS: Then put your hand in mine. AN.: Yes, Father. Here.
OEDIPUS: If I should trust you, set my mind at rest;
        Let me forsake my refuge without fear.

CHORUS:
        No one will force you to leave against your will.
OEDIPUS: Shall I come closer? CH.: Yes. Closer to me.
OEDIPUS: Is that enough? CH.: Daughter, you see   170
        What the old man needs to do. Lead him nearer still.
ANTIGONE: Let me guide you, Father. Your steps are dark.

                    *   *   *

CHORUS: Stranger, we pity your wretched state.
            You must learn to obey a foreign law:
            To hate what the city has come to hate,
                To revere what we hold in awe.

OEDIPUS: So then, to some undedicated spot
        Lead me, my child, for there I shall be free
            To speak to them and listen. Let us not
        Wage war in vain against necessity.   180

CHORUS:
        Do not leave the bounds of the ledge beneath your feet.
OEDIPUS: Nearer than this? CH.: No. Take care.
OEDIPUS: Shall I sit down? CH.: Beside you there,
        Is the level edge of the rock. Let that be your seat.
ANTIGONE: Come, Father, come! Lean on my arm.
            Walk where I walk—here—follow me.
            My love will protect your age from harm.
OEDIPUS: How can such pain, such suffering be?
CHORUS: Rest, rest. Long was the road you came,
            In misery, holding another's hand.   190
            But tell us now of your race, your name,
            And the name of your native land.

OEDIPUS:
            I have no native land! But do not seek—
CHORUS: Seek what, old man? What is it that you have forbidden?
OEDIPUS: Do not seek to know who I am. Let my birth be hidden.
CHORUS: What do you mean? OE.: It was dreadful, dreadful!
                CH.: Speak!
OEDIPUS: How can I speak? What evil, child, is in store?
CHORUS: Tell us! Who are you? Who was your father? Who?
OEDIPUS: Daughter! What more must I now endure, what more?
ANTIGONE: They drive you to the brink, and they must hear.   200
OEDIPUS: Yes, I must tell them. I must make it clear.

CHORUS: Answer us! Speak! You are talking too long, you two!

OEDIPUS: You have heard of Laius (CH. *cries out*), of Oedipus—
CH.: Oedipus! You!

OEDIPUS: Do not fear—(*clamor continues*) I am lost! Antigone!
What will they do?

CHORUS: Go! Go! Out with you! Out of our country! Go!

OEDIPUS: You gave me your word! Will you prove to your word untrue?

CHORUS:
We do you no wrong. We give back again
Evil for evil, trick for trick.
You were false to us. Your reward is pain.
Up, up! Be quick!
You pollute the city in which you stay!
Off with you! Go your way!

ANTIGONE:
You are compassionate. And you. And you.
You have heard of my father, heard the tale that is told
Of the deeds he never meant to do;
And you cannot pity him, though he is blind and old.
Have pity, then, on me!
On me, here pleading with you face to face.
My eyes are as clear as yours are; I might be
A child of your own race.
For my father, only for him I plead.
Be mindful of him in his need.
You are like gods to us. We stand before you
In supplication and in fear.
By your wife, your child, by the god whom you revere,
By your most prized possession I implore you:
Grant us your mercy, let us hear
Words that we scarcely hope to have you say.
What mortal is there who can disobey
A god who leads the way?

CHORUS:
Truly, my child, we pity both of you
For both have suffered; but because we fear
The judgment of the gods, we can say nothing
Beyond what we have said to you already.

OEDIPUS:
What is fame worth or golden reputation,
When no good comes of it? Men say that Athens,
Above all cities, reverences the gods,
Above all cities, shelters the afflicted,

Offers the stranger refuge and defends him.
And have I found these qualities in Athens?   240
You made me quit my rocky seat, and now
You drive me from the land, fearing my name,
My name alone. What else have you to fear?
Not my own person, not what I have done.
You shrink from me because of my father and mother,
But I know this: if I could tell their story,
Then you would see I did not act myself
So much as I endured the acts of others.
Was I by nature evil? Was I a sinner,
I who repaid an injury done to me?   250
If I had acted knowingly, even then
You could not think me wrong; but I knew nothing.
All that I did I did in ignorance.
They at whose hands I suffered meant to kill me.
Since you have drawn me from my sanctuary,
Sirs, by the gods, I beg you to protect me.
How can you honor them when you refuse
To pay them due respect? The gods look down
Alike upon the pious and the impious.
Remember that not one irreverent man   260
Ever escaped them. May they help you now!
Lest you should darken the bright fame of Athens
By doing unholy deeds. You have received me,
A suppliant who trusted in your pledge.
Deliver me from my peril; guard me well.
Do not despise me when you see my face
Disfigured as it is; for I am holy,
Under the gods' protection, and I have come
To bring a blessing to the people here.
When I have spoken to your lord the King,   270
You will have heard all and will understand.
Until he comes, take care you do not harm me.

CHORUS:

Sir, these are matters of a fearful import.
We feel the weight of what you urge upon us,
And are content to let the King pass judgment.

OEDIPUS:

Where is the ruler of this country, strangers?

CHORUS:

In the city where his father once was king.
The man who summoned us has gone to bring him.

OEDIPUS:

Will he have consideration for a blind man?
Will he care enough, do you think, to come himself?   280

CHORUS:

Yes, he will come, when he has heard your name.

OEDIPUS:

Who is there that could give him such a message?

CHORUS:

The road is long, and every traveler
Helps to spread rumors. When they reach the King,
You can be certain that he will not linger,
For every land has learned your name, old man.
Even if he is resting or asleep,
When once he hears of you he will come quickly.

OEDIPUS:

And may his coming here bring happiness
No less to his own city than to me! 290
For so a good man benefits himself.

ANTIGONE:

Father! Can it be true? Do I dare say it?

OEDIPUS:

What is the matter, child? AN.: I see a woman
Coming in our direction. She is riding
A colt of Etna; a Thessalian hat
Keeps the sun off her face. I think I know her.
No, I am wrong. Yes! It is she, it is!
I see her radiant look as she comes closer.
Ismene! Our Ismene! She is here!

OEDIPUS:

Do you mean it? AN.: Yes, your daughter and my sister.
A minute longer and her voice will tell you.

Enter ISMENE

ISMENE:

Father! Sister! The sweetest of all names.
How hard it was, how hard it was to find you!
And now I can scarcely see you through my tears.

OEDIPUS:

Child, are you here? IS.: You have suffered, Father, suffered!

OEDIPUS:

Ismene, have you come? IS.: A weary journey.

OEDIPUS:

Touch me, my daughter. IS.: Each of you take my hand.

OEDIPUS:

Children, children! IS.: How miserable a life!

OEDIPUS:

Her life and mine? IS.: I am the third in sorrow.

OEDIPUS:

  Why have you come here? is.: To look after you.   310

OEDIPUS:

  Anxious to see me? is.: Yes, and to bring you news.

  I came with the only servant I could trust.

OEDIPUS:

  Now that we need their help, where are your brothers?

ISMENE:

  They are both—where they are. False! Treacherous!

OEDIPUS:

  Their lives are copies of the life in Egypt!

  Where men at home sit weaving, while the women

  Go out to earn the family's daily bread.

  As for you, children, those whose task it was

  To help me bear my burden stay indoors,

  Tending the house like girls, while in their place 320

  You share these miseries. Antigone,

  Ever since you outgrew the childish years

  That needed care, and came to womanhood,

  You led me, old and weary, on my journeys.

  Time after time you roamed the savage forest,

  Hungry and barefoot. Time after time you suffered

  From drenching rain and the fierce heat of the sun,

  Giving no thought to home with all its comforts

  So that your father might not be neglected.

  Ismene, you stole out of Thebes unnoticed, 330

  Bringing the oracles that the gods had uttered

  Concerning me. And you assumed the office

  Of faithful sentinel on my behalf,

  When I was being driven from the land.

  What brought you here? What is your news this time?

  You are not empty-handed. I am certain

  You have a message that I dread to hear.

ISMENE:

  Father, what I endured in seeking you

  I will not speak of. I have no wish to suffer

  A second time in making known my hardships. 340

  But the evil that has come upon your sons,

  Your ill-starred sons—this is the news I bring.

  At first, when they considered in cold blood

  The ancestral curse that had not loosed its hold

  On your unhappy house, they were content

  To give the throne to Creon, that the city

  Might not become unclean. But now, some god

  And their own evil minds have maddened them,

  Rousing them to a sinful rivalry

  For the title and authority of king. 350

Polyneices has been driven from his throne,
And from the country, by his younger brother.
And it is rumored that he now has fled
For refuge to the vale of Argos. There
He makes a new alliance by his marriage
And raises up an army of new friends.
He means to have proud Argos conquer Thebes
Or lift up Thebes triumphant to the stars.
This is not idle fancy; they have done
These fearful deeds. But where the gods will bring   360
Your sorrows to an end I cannot tell.

OEDIPUS:
My sorrows! Can you hope the gods will ever
Appoint a time for my deliverance?

ISMENE:
Yes. The new oracle has given me hope.

OEDIPUS:
What oracle, child? What has been prophesied?

ISMENE:
That before long our countrymen will seek you,
Living or dead, to safeguard their own welfare.

OEDIPUS:
And who could benefit from such as I am?

ISMENE:
You have become the source of Theban strength.

OEDIPUS:
When I am helpless, do I become a man?   370

ISMENE:
The gods who struck you down now lift you up.

OEDIPUS:
To ruin youth and honor age is petty.

ISMENE:
And yet because this oracle has been spoken
Creon will not be long in coming here.

OEDIPUS:
Why will he come, Ismene? Can you tell me?

ISMENE:
To get you within their grasp and then to keep you
Close to their land, where you may not set foot.

OEDIPUS:
How can I be of help outside their borders?

ISMENE:
If they neglect your tomb, they will be cursed.

OEDIPUS:
That truth we know without a god to tell us.   380

ISMENE:

And so they want you near them, in a place
Where you will not be free from their control.

OEDIPUS:

At least they will bury me in Theban earth.

ISMENE:

They cannot. You have shed your father's blood.

OEDIPUS:

Then they shall never have me in their power!

ISMENE:

Someday this will be hard for Thebes to bear.

OEDIPUS:

When will that happen? What will cause it, child?

ISMENE:

Your anger, when they stand beside your tomb.

OEDIPUS:

Where did you hear what you are telling me?

ISMENE:

From the ambassadors to the shrine of Delphi.   390

OEDIPUS:

That was Apollo's prophecy? You are certain?

ISMENE:

So the men said when they returned to Thebes.

OEDIPUS:

Have either of your brothers heard of this?

ISMENE:

Yes, both of them; they understand it well.

OEDIPUS:

So then, those scoundrels, knowing what they did,
Cared more for kingship than for my return!

ISMENE:

Your words are terrible, but they are true.

OEDIPUS:

May the gods grant the blaze be not extinguished!
The blaze they kindled when they took up arms
In the war that was their portion. May the outcome   400
Rest in my hands alone! Were I the judge,
He who is king now should be king no longer;
He who is exiled should remain in exile.
When I, their father, was proclaimed an outlaw,
When I was driven shamefully from my home
And banished from my country, they did nothing—
Nothing to hinder it, nothing to help me.
The city acted rightly, you will say,
In granting me what I myself desired.
No. I did not desire it. When my soul,   410

On that first day, was shaken by a tempest,
When death by stoning was my dearest wish,
I could find none to give me what I longed for.
And later when my anguish was allayed,
And I began to feel that my misdeeds
Had been too heavily punished by my passion,
Then was it that the city, long delaying,
Drove me away by force. And my two sons,
Who could have helped their father, would not help him,
Would not so much as speak a single word,   420
But let me wander forth, from that time forward
A homeless outcast brought to beggary.
These two, these daughters, have done everything
That women could do. They have given me
Food, a safe shelter, filial loyalty:
While their two brothers, turning against their father,
Snatched at the throne and scepter of a king.
Never shall they win Oedipus for an ally!
Never shall any benefit come to them
From ruling over Thebes! That I am sure of   430
Now that I hear Ismene's oracles,
And now that I consider those of old,
Those that Apollo has fulfilled at last.
Therefore, let them send Creon after me,
Creon or any Theban who has power.
Because if you are willing to assist me—
You, strangers, with your great protectresses,
The dreadful goddesses who guard your land—
You will secure deliverance for yourselves
And bring disaster on my enemies.   440

CHORUS:

You and your daughters waken our compassion.
Your misery and your saying you can save us
Prompt me to counsel you for your own good.

OEDIPUS:

Sir, you are kind. I will accept your guidance.

CHORUS:

Then make atonement to those deities
Whose ground you trespassed on when you first came here.

OEDIPUS:

What are the ceremonies? Tell me, stranger.

CHORUS:

First cleanse your hands, then bring for the libation
The water of an ever-flowing spring.

OEDIPUS:

And when I have clear water, then what follows?   450

CHORUS:

> You will find bowls of cunning workmanship.
> Cover the rims and the handles on each side.

OEDIPUS:

> What shall I use? Young branches? Woolen fabrics?

CHORUS:

> You will be given lamb's wool, newly shorn.

OEDIPUS:

> And after that, how is the rite completed?

CHORUS:

> Face toward the dawn and pour out your libations.

OEDIPUS:

> Using the bowls that you have spoken of?

CHORUS:

> Yes, but the third one must be wholly emptied.

OEDIPUS:

> What offering do I pour from this last bowl?

CHORUS:

> Water and honey, but with no wine added.　　　　　　460

OEDIPUS:

> The shadowed earth will swallow it. What next?

CHORUS:

> Using both hands, lay on the ground thrice nine
> Branches of olive, while you pronounce your prayer.

OEDIPUS:

> Say what it is, for it concerns me greatly.

CHORUS:

> You, or whoever acts in your behalf,
> Should pray those powers whose name is the Benignant
> To give a suppliant their benign protection.
> Speak softly, do not raise your voice. Then go
> Without a backward glance. If you do this,
> I will take courage and come to your defence;　　　　470
> Otherwise, Oedipus, I fear for you.

OEDIPUS:

> Children, you heard the advice of those who live here?

ANTIGONE:

> Yes, we have heard. Tell us what we must do.

OEDIPUS:

> I cannot go. I bear a double burden,
> Blindness and lack of strength. One of you two
> Go and discharge those duties. I am sure
> One loyal, faithful soul before the shrine
> Makes ample satisfaction for ten thousand.
> Go quickly, then; but do not leave me helpless.
> How can I move without a hand to guide me?　　　　480

ISMENE:

> Father, I will perform these ceremonies,
> When someone tells me where to find the place.

CHORUS:

> There, on the far side of the grove, my child.
> If you need anything, a guard will help you.

ISMENE:

> Then I will go. Antigone, stay here
> To help our father. Nothing we do for him,
> However hard, can ever be called hardship.

Exit ISMENE

CHORUS:

> It is dreadful, sir, to waken long-slumbering sorrow,
> Yet high are our hopes that the truth will be told at last.

OE.: What now? CH.: Of your anguish beyond all relief, all cure, 490
> The grief that has held you fast.

OE.: As a stranger, a guest I implore you not to uncover
> The shame I have had to endure.

CH.: Wide-spread is the story and grows no less in the telling,
> Let us hear it rightly told; we are eager to learn.

OE.: Have mercy! CH.: Be patient, sir. OE.: No! CH.: We did all
> that you asked for.
> Do this in your turn.

OE.: Of the deeds that have brought me to misery none was intended.
> Be Zeus my witness! Not one of them all, not one!

CH.: What were they? OE.: The Thebans gave me, unknowing,
> a bride, 500
> A curse that I could not shun.

CH.: Can the tale as we heard it be true: that your marriage was shameful,
> That your mother lay by your side?

OE.: You stab me! Your words are cruel as death to me, stranger.
> And these daughters, these two—how fearful a thing to tell!—

CH.: Your daughters! OE.: My scourges! CH.: No! Never!
> OE.: The mother who bore them
> Bore me as well.

CH.: Their mother and yours you wed!
> Then these are your daughters and— OE.: Sisters! Their father's
> sisters!

CH.: Horrible! OE.: Countless horrors recoil on my head. 510

CH.: You have suffered— OE.: As much as a man can bear.

CH.: What you did— OE.: I did nothing. CH.: Nothing! OE.: No. I
> was given
> A gift by the Thebans—would I had never deserved it—
> A gift of grief beyond compare.

CH.:   There is more than we long to know.
Is it true you are stained with blood? OE.: Why, why do you ask me?
CH.:   With the blood of your father? OE.: You strike me blow after
         blow!
CH.:   You killed him! OE.: Yes, killed him! And yet I am sure—
CH.: Sure of what? OE.: Of my innocence. CH.: No! OE.: Of what
        crime am I guilty?
    I saved my own life, I killed the men who attacked me.   520
       I have fallen this low, but my hands are pure.

CHORUS:

    Our King is coming—Theseus, the son of Aegeus.
    Your message, sir, has summoned him to help you.

Enter THESEUS

THESEUS:

    I know you, son of Laius; for long ago
    I heard of the bloody act that blinded you,
    And I have learned still more from what was told me
    As I was coming here. Your clothes, your face,
    Scarred and disfigured, show me who you are.
    Such misery as yours moves my compassion.
    What suit to Athens or to me has brought you   530
    Into our presence, with the unhappy girl
    Who stands beside you there? Make known your purpose.
    You could not tell me of a fate so fearful
    That I would stand aloof—I who remember
    That in my childhood I too was an exile,
    And that no man has risked his life so often
    As I in my encounters in far lands.
    I could not turn away from anyone
    Like you, a stranger, or refuse to help him.
    I know well, being mortal, that my claim   540
    Upon the future is no more than yours.

OEDIPUS:

    Theseus, the kindness of your words is kingly,
    So that I need say little. You spoke the truth
    About my name, my parentage, and my country.
    Nothing remains for me except to say
    What my desire is, and my tale is told.

THESEUS:

    I am eager to learn what you would have me do.

OEDIPUS:

    I have come here to offer you a gift:
    My old, worn, ugly body. Yet it brings you
    Far greater benefit than beauty could.   550

THESEUS:

    What benefit can you say your body brings?

OEDIPUS:

    You shall learn later, but not yet, I think.

THESEUS:

    When will it finally be made known to us?

OEDIPUS:

    When I am dead and you have buried me.

THESEUS:

    You set your heart upon the close of life,
    Forgetting or ignoring the years between.

OEDIPUS:

    Yes, but the close will gather in life's harvest.

THESEUS:

    Why then, the favor that you ask is small.

OEDIPUS:

    And yet my burial is no slight issue.

THESEUS:

    Because it lies between your sons and me?   560

OEDIPUS:

    Theseus, they hope to take me back to Thebes.

THESEUS:

    Then it is wrong for you to stay in exile.

OEDIPUS:

    No, no! When I was willing, they refused.

THESEUS:

    As matters stand with you, anger is foolish.

OEDIPUS:

    Bear with me now. Reprove me when you have heard me.

THESEUS:

    Speak. I must not pass judgment without knowledge.

OEDIPUS:

    I have suffered, Theseus, wrong after bitter wrong.

THESEUS:

    You mean the ancient curse upon your race?

OEDIPUS:

    No. All the land has echoed with that story.

THESEUS:

    What is it then? Some more than mortal grief?   570

OEDIPUS:

    My life has come to this: I have been driven
    From Thebes by my two sons, and am condemned
    To life-long exile as a parricide.

THESEUS:

    Then how can they bring you back from banishment?

OEDIPUS:

    The oracle of the gods will force them to.

103

THESEUS:

> What has been prophesied to rouse their fear?

OEDIPUS:

> That here in Athens they will be struck down.

THESEUS:

> What bitterness could ever come between us?

OEDIPUS:

> Dear son of Aegeus, only the gods themselves
> Are free from age or death. All else is ruined   580
> By overmastering time. The strength of earth,
> The strength of the body, both alike decay.
> Faith dies, and lack of faith comes into being.
> And friendship between men and between cities
> Is but a breath that blows unsteadily;
> For all discover that love turns to hatred,
> And that from hatred love springs up anew.
> The sky is cloudless over Thebes and Athens,
> Yet time in its endless course will bring to birth
> Unnumbered nights and days, and one of these   590
> Will mark the moment when, for some slight word,
> Their swords will cut this concord into shreds;
> And when my body in its sleep of death,
> Cold in the grave, will drink up their warm blood,
> If Zeus be Zeus and Phoebus a true prophet.
> But these are mysteries that I must not speak of.
> Let what I say end with my first request.
> Make good your promise to me. Then you will find
> Profit in letting me live here in your land,
> Unless the gods intend to play me false.   600

CHORUS:

> Sir, from the first, this man has shown himself
> Willing and able to do good to us.

THESEUS:

> Then surely we must not reject the friendship
> Of such a man as this. He is our ally,
> To whom we owe our hospitality
> By mutual right. Moreover, he has come
> As a suppliant to our goddesses, and brings
> No small return to Athens and to me.
> I reverence these claims, and I accept
> The favor which he offers. I will make him   610
> A citizen of our country. If he wishes
> To stay with you, I charge you to protect him.
> Or it may please you better, Oedipus,
> To come with me to Athens. You need only
> Make your decision, and I am satisfied.

OEDIPUS:
>   Zeus, look with favor on such men as this!
THESEUS:
>   What is your pleasure, sir? To go with me?
OEDIPUS:
>   If it were lawful, yes. But this is the place—
THESEUS:
>   What must you do here? I will not oppose you.
OEDIPUS:
>   Here I shall vanquish those who have cast me out.   620
THESEUS:
>   Your presence here brings promise of great good.
OEDIPUS:
>   Yes, good, if you are faithful to your pledge.
THESEUS:
>   You need not fear that I shall ever fail you.
OEDIPUS:
>   I will exact no oath. You are not false.
THESEUS:
>   An oath could be no better than my word.
OEDIPUS:
>   But how, how will you help?   TH.: What frightens you?
OEDIPUS:
>   They will come here—TH.: These friends will take care of that.
OEDIPUS:
>   But if you leave me—TH.: I know what I must do.
OEDIPUS:
>   There is good cause for fear—TH.: I am not fearful.
OEDIPUS:
>   You do not know the threats—TH.: I know this much: 630
>   No one shall take you away against my will.
>   How often loud and empty threats break out
>   In sudden anger! But as soon as reason
>   Asserts its mastery, they come to nothing.
>   As for the Thebans, though they have plucked up courage
>   To menace you with talk of your abduction,
>   Yet they will find the seas that stretch between us
>   Too wide and stormy for their navigation.
>   Take heart, sir. For aside from my resolve
>   To shelter you, Apollo has been your guide.   640
>   And yet, I think, though I am not here myself,
>   My name will be sufficient to protect you.

>   *Exit* THESEUS

CHORUS:

    Noble the breed of horses here
In white Colonus, the land of our birth,
The loveliest land in all the earth.
    A distant music, pure and clear,
Rises from green, secluded vales:
The constant trill of the nightingales
    Deep in their haunts of tangled vine,
    Of sacred ivy, dark as wine.   650
Thick is the god's inviolate wood,
    Rich in berries and rich in fruit.
    The sun is curtained, the wind is mute.
    Here Dionysus makes his home;
    And reveling with him, forever roam
The nymphs who nursed him in babyhood.

    Daily by heavenly dew is fed
The narcissus, that the immortals wear
In crowning clusters on their hair.
    And here the crocus lifts its head,   660
Spreading abroad its golden gleam.
And all year long a brimming stream,
    Fed by fountains that never fail,
    Winds on its way through hill and dale,
Down to the broad and swelling plains,
    With its crystal current evermore
    Quickening the soil's abundant store.
    To the Muses' choir is the country dear;
    And Aphrodite has lingered here,
Goddess who rides with the golden reins.   670

Here is a marvel unheard of elsewhere,
    Here only the grey-leaved olive grows
Self-renewed, invincible, nurse of our children,
    A thing of terror to all our foes.
Wide through the land spread its hallowed branches,
    By the hands of youth and of age unmarred,
A tree that Zeus's unsleeping vision
    And Pallas Athene's grey eyes guard.

Praised be the might of Athens, our mother:
    The splendid gift that a god confers.   680
She is famed for her colts, for the breed of her horses;
    And dominion over the sea is hers.
Our Lord Poseidon established her glory
    When he fashioned the bridle that tames the steed,
When he fashioned the oar that leaps to follow
    Where the dancing feet of the sea-nymphs lead.

ANTIGONE:

>You have been praised above all lands, Colonus!
>Let what you do now be as glorious.

OEDIPUS:

>Antigone! What is it? AN.: It is Creon.
>Father, he is not coming here alone.   690

OEDIPUS:

>Friends! Friends! You are kind-hearted, all of you!
>Bring me, I beg you, to the goal of safety!

CHORUS:

>Take courage. You shall be safe. Though we are old,
>Colonus still has all the strength of youth.

Enter CREON *and other Thebans*

CREON:

>I see that you are the elders of this country
>And that my coming here has frightened you,
>But do not shrink from me or speak in anger.
>I have not come with any violent purpose.
>I am an old man. Furthermore, I know
>That in all Hellas there is no mightier city   700
>Than this that I have come to. Old as I am,
>I have been sent to plead with him, to beg him
>To go with me, back to the land of Cadmus.
>I am the envoy, not of one man alone,
>But of the whole of Thebes since, as his kinsman,
>I felt more sorrow than the rest could feel
>For his great sufferings. Then hear me, sir.
>Unhappy Oedipus, come home with us.
>All the Cadmean race, as is their right,
>Are summoning you, and I above them all.   710
>For unless I am the basest man in the world,
>I in particular must pity you,
>When I see you as you are: a life-long stranger,
>Old, wretched, drifting, destitute, untended
>Except for this one girl. I never thought
>She could have fallen to such a depth as this—
>Poor child! the nurse of what you have become,
>Leading a life of beggary, still young
>And still unmarried, a prize for the first comer.
>This is a harsh reproof, hateful to utter.   720
>We are involved—you, I, and all our race—
>In open shame that cannot be concealed.
>Therefore, by your ancestral gods I beg you
>To bring it to an end. Oedipus, hear me!

Come back to your fathers' house, your fathers' city.
Part from this land in friendship; she deserves it.
But your own country, your nurse of long ago,
Has the first claim upon your piety.

OEDIPUS:
Creon, is there nothing you shrink from doing?
Your cunning can take any plea and turn   730
Its justice into trickery! Do you hope
To lure me a second time into a trap
Where I would touch the depth of misery?
Once, long ago, when I was sick with the anguish
That I myself had brought upon my head,
When my one passionate wish was to be exiled,
You could not bring yourself to show me kindness.
But later, when the storm had spent itself,
When it seemed sweet to me to live at home,
That was the moment that you chose to drive me   740
Out of my house, out of my country. Then
You were untouched by any claim of kinship.
But when you see how warmly I am welcomed
By Athens and her people, you undertake
To draw me away again, with gentle words
Hiding your cruel purpose. Who takes pleasure
In kindness done to him against his will?
For if a man denied you what you longed for,
Refused his help until you had found already
Full satisfaction for your needs, his offer   750
Would be worth nothing. Your deceitful offer
Is worth no more. And to make plain your falsehood,
I will tell all men here what you intend:
You have not come to take me home again
But only to bring me to the Theban border.
There you would keep me to prevent our city
From being harmed by Athens. But that lot
Is not for you. Another is: my curse
To haunt the country. And this is my sons' portion
Of their inheritance: a place to die in.   760
Is not my knowledge of Theban destiny
Truer than yours? Its sources are more unerring:
Apollo and his father, Zeus himself.
You come to me with falsehood upon your lips
And with a hard, keen edge upon your tongue;
And yet your words do you more harm than good.
But well I know that I can never convince you.
Leave us alone! Go! Even as we are,
Patience would make our life here not unhappy.

CREON:

> Do you think that such an outcome of our meeting 770
> Will injure me more than it injures you?

OEDIPUS:

> Nothing could be so sweet as to have you fail
> With everyone here, as you have failed with me.

CREON:

> Must your life prove that long years bring no wisdom?
> Will not your wretchedness disgrace old age?

OEDIPUS:

> Your tongue is clever, but I know of no one
> Who can be always fluent and yet honest.

CREON:

> Yes, fluency is often out of place.

OEDIPUS:

> You mean your words were brief and to the point!

CREON:

> Not for a man with as little sense as you. 780

OEDIPUS:

> Creon, I speak for all of us. Be off!
> Recall your sentinels. Watch me no longer.
> This is the spot where I was meant to stay.

CREON:

> Men of Colonus, be witness to his behavior.
> (*to* OEDIPUS) You I have done with. As for the way you speak
> To your own kindred, if I get hold of you—

OEDIPUS:

> No one gets hold of me. Here are my friends and allies.

CREON:

> You will soon suffer. There are other ways.

OEDIPUS:

> Threats! Boasts! How do you hope to make them good?

CREON:

> How? Through your daughters: one has been seized already 790
> And sent away; the other will soon be taken.

OEDIPUS:

> No! No! CR.: What! Crying? You will cry louder soon.

OEDIPUS:

> Friends! Friends! Help! Help! Do not forsake me friends!
> He is guilty of sacrilege! Drive him from the land!

CHORUS:

> Go, Creon, go! What you have done already
> And what you are doing now is wickedness.

CREON (*to* GUARDS):

> You. It is time now. Seize her. Carry her off,
> Unless she is willing to go of her own accord.

(ANTIGONE *turning to fly*):

Lost! Lost! They are everywhere! No one can save me. No one!
Not even a god! CH.: What are you doing, Creon?   800

CREON:

I will not touch him, but the woman is mine.

OEDIPUS:

Elders! Princes! CH.: Creon, you have no right.

CREON:

I have. CH.: How so? CR.: I take what belongs to me.

OEDIPUS:

Athens! Athens!

CHORUS: Stop! Let her go! We shall see who is stronger!

CREON: Keep away! CH.: Not from you while she still is your prisoner.

CREON: Athens and Thebes are at war if you touch me.

OEDIPUS: I foretold this would happen! CH.: Release her this moment!
Free her, I tell you! CR.: Be quiet! have you power to
command me?

CHORUS: Set her at liberty! CR.: (*to* GUARDS) Off with you. Follow
your orders.   810

CHORUS: Athenians! Countrymen! Save us!
Our city, our land is dishonored!
Come to our rescue!

ANTIGONE:

Friends! Friends! They have taken me prisoner! Help me! Help!

OEDIPUS:

Where are you, Antigone? AN.: Here! They are dragging
me off!

OEDIPUS:

Give me your hand! AN.: I cannot. I am helpless.

CREON (*to* GUARDS):

Take her away. Be off. OE.: Oh! How I suffer!

Exeunt GUARDS *and* ANTIGONE

CREON:

So, in your wanderings you will never again
Have those two staffs to lean on. You had hoped
To triumph over your country and your friends,   820
Whose orders I obey, prince though I am.
Well then, enjoy your triumph. Yet in time
You will come to see that now, as in the past,
To turn against your friends does you no good.
Always you have been cursed by your quick temper.

CHORUS:

Stop, Creon, stop! CR.: Keep your hands off, I tell you!

CHORUS (*seizing him*):
>Not while those two girls are your prisoners.

CREON (*throwing them off*):
>In that case I will carry off to Thebes
>More than his daughters as security.

CHORUS:
>What are you going to do? CR.: Seize Oedipus.   830

CHORUS:
>A fearful threat! CR.: No, not a threat, a fact—
>Unless, perhaps, your King will come to stop me.

OEDIPUS:
>What shameless words! Will you lay hands on me?

CREON:
>Be still! OE.: No! Goddesses, dread guardians!
>Grant that I may utter this one curse.
>This fiend has torn away the helpless girl
>Who was my eyesight when these eyes were dark.
>Therefore, thou Sun-god, all-beholding Helios,
>Hear thou my prayer: may he and all his race
>In their old age lead such a life as mine.   840

CREON:
>Be witnesses of that, men of Colonus.

OEDIPUS:
>They see us both. They know what you have done,
>And know that my revenge is only breath.

CREON:
>I cannot contain myself! I am alone
>And slow with age, but I will take him with me.

OEDIPUS:
>How can I bear it?

CHORUS: Have you boldness enough to suppose you can do it?

CREON: Yes, I have. CH.: Then is Athens a city no longer.

CREON: With justice to arm them the weak are triumphant.

OEDIPUS: Do you hear what he threatens? CH.: Zeus knows it
>shall never   850
>Be put into practice. CR.: Zeus knows, but not you. You
>know nothing.

CHORUS: Insolence! Insolence! CR.: Yes. But you have to endure it.

CHORUS: Citizens! Citizens! Princes!
>Follow them! After them quickly!
>Make for the border!

Enter THESEUS *with* ATTENDANTS

THESEUS:
>What do you want? Your shouting has cut short
>My sacrifice before the sea-god's altar.

What has been happening? Let me know the trouble
That has brought me here too quickly for my comfort.

OEDIPUS:

My friend! I know your voice. I am wronged, wronged! 860

THESEUS:

How? Who has done you wrong? Speak, Oedipus.

OEDIPUS:

That man there, Creon. He has carried off
My last remaining children, my two daughters.

THESEUS:

What! OE.: Yes, it is true. Creon has taken them.

THESEUS (*to* ATTENDANTS):

One of you there. Quick! Go back to the altars.
Break off the sacrifice. Have them start out—
Everyone, horse and foot—at their top speed
To where the roads fork. If the women are lost,
I will become this stranger's laughingstock,
Beaten by brute strength. Go, I tell you! Quickly! 870

Exit ATTENDANT

As for that man, if I had let myself
Treat him as he deserves, he would have felt
The violence of my anger. But instead,
He shall be subject to the kind of law
That he himself has brought here. (*to* CREON) You shall never
Leave Athens until those women stand before me.
What you have done is a disgrace to me,
To those of your own blood, and to your country.
You have come to a land always upholding justice,
Sanctioning nothing without recourse to law; 880
And yet you have slighted our authority,
Burst in upon us, seized and carried away
Whoever took your fancy, as if you thought
That there were no men left within my city,
Or only slaves, and I was a mere nothing.
Thebes did not teach you this outrageous conduct.
To breed rebellious sons is not her custom;
Nor would she praise you if she saw you now,
Robbing me, yes, robbing the gods themselves
By kidnapping their wretched suppliants. 890
If I were standing now on Theban soil,
I would not drag off anything by force,
However just my claim to it might be,
Without your ruler's sanction. I would know
How I, as a foreigner, should live among you.

You bring dishonor upon an innocent city,
Your own Thebes; and although you have lived long,
You are still stupid. I have told you once,
And I tell you again now: bring his daughters back
Without delay, unless you wish to live   900
Among us as an alien, a forced guest.
These are not merely words. My heart is in them.

CHORUS:

You hear that, stranger? That is our judgment of you;
Your land is noble and your deeds are base.

CREON:

Theseus, how could I ever think that Athens
Lacked manliness or wisdom? I supposed
Her citizens would never be so eager
To serve my kinsmen as to shelter them
Against my will. This country, I was certain,
Would show no hospitality to a man   910
Steeped in pollution: the slayer of his father,
And partner of an unholy marriage-bed,
Mother with son. Knowing the Hill of Ares
Makes wise decisions and does not allow
Such vagabonds to stay here, I felt free
To seize this prize. Yet I would not have touched him
If he had not called down a bitter curse
On me and on my race, an injury
Which justified, I thought, my giving back
Evil for evil. Anger does not grow old;   920
Only the dead escape the sting of it.
You can, of course, act any way you choose,
For I am helpless, though my cause is just.
Yet I will do my best, old as I am,
To follow the example that you set me.

OEDIPUS:

What bare-faced insolence, Creon! Whose old age
Do you think has been dishonored, yours or mine?
You have poured out a stream of accusations:
Murder and incest, all the disastrous things
That my hard fate has forced me to endure.   930
So the gods willed it, nursing their long displeasure,
Doubtless, against my house. For I myself
Cannot be charged with any deliberate crime
For which, as retribution, I was driven
To sin against my parents and myself.
Tell me. If through some oracle my father
Was destined to be slain by his own son,
Could I be justly blamed—I, not yet born,

113

Not yet so much as begotten or conceived?
And if, being born at last to bear this burden,   940
I met my father, not knowing who he was,
Quarreled, and killed him without intending to,
What sin attaches to this ignorant act?
As for my mother—how contemptible!—
Do you feel no shame in forcing me to speak
As I now must of her—of your own sister—
And of her marriage; for your words have gone
Beyond the bounds of piety. My mother!
Yes it was she—what bitterness!—who in shame
Bore children to the child that she had borne,   950
Though neither she nor I knew what we did.
One thing at least I know—that you are ready
To slander us, for of my own free will
I did not marry, nor of my own free will
Do I now speak. I cannot be thought guilty.
Not in this marriage. Not in my father's murder
That you are forever throwing in my teeth.
Answer me this one question that I ask you.
If, here and now, someone came up to you
And tried to kill you—you, the innocent Creon—   960
What would you do? Inquire if he was your father,
Or strike back instantly? Loving your life,
You would, I am sure, repay him blow for blow
Without a long search for your legal sanction.
Yet that was the catastrophe I encountered,
Led by the gods. If he could live again,
My father himself would not deny the truth
Of what I say. But you—lacking all sense
Of fitness, babbling, making no distinction
Between what should and what should not be talked of—   970
You, here in public, heap your insults on me.
And this, you think, is the proper time to flatter
The famous Theseus and to proclaim how well
The Athenian state is governed. Yet in giving
Such lavish praises, you forget that Athens
Excels in reverent worship of the gods;
For you had planned to abduct me, an old man
Who had sought the gods' protection. You have seized
My daughters and have tried to seize me also.
Hence, I invoke these goddesses, with prayers   980
Beseeching them to come to my assistance,
To fight in my defence, that you may learn
What manner of men they are who guard this city.

CHORUS:

Sir, Oedipus, our guest, has been accurst;
Yet he is innocent and deserves our help.

THESEUS:

We have talked enough. Those who have done this violence
Hurry away, and we, their victims, stand here.

CREON:

What orders have you for a helpless man?

THESEUS:

These. Lead us after them. Take me along.
If you have kept his daughters in this country,   990
Show me where I can find them. But if your men
Are carrying off their prize, we need not trouble.
Others will catch them. They will never thank
Their gods for their escape from Athens. Come!
Lead on! The captor is made captive; fortune
Has snared the hunter; no ill-gotten gains
Can be kept long. But do not expect your helper;
For daring and insolent though you are, I know
You did not undertake this singlehanded.
No, you had some accomplice whom you trusted   1000
When you came here. He must be hunted down.
Athens must be the master and not he.
Can you grasp any part of what I have said?
Or do you think you can ignore my words,
As you ignored those warnings that you heard
When you first put your scheming into practice?

CREON:

Whatever you say here I shall not object to.
When I am home, I shall know how to act.

THESEUS:

Threaten me if you want, but lead the way.
Now, Oedipus, you can stay here in peace   1010
With my assurance that, unless I die,
I will restore your children to your hands.

OEDIPUS:

You have acted nobly, Theseus. May the gods
Reward you for the kindness you have shown me.

Exeunt THESEUS, CREON, *and* ATTENDANTS

CHORUS:

Would we were there in the clamor of battle!
There where the enemy, wheeling to meet us,
     Takes up his stand;
Perhaps at the shore beloved by Apollo,
Perhaps where the two great goddesses hallow
     The torch-lit sand,   1020

Whose priest, performing their awful service,
Locks their votaries' lips in silence.
War-waking Theseus will come on the captives,
Will free the two sisters while shouts of his warriors
  Ring through the land.

Perhaps to the west of the snows of Mount Oea,
Racing their chariots, urging their horses,
  Headlong they flee.
Creon will fail! Those who follow King Theseus
Are mighty in battle, and we of Colonus,   1030
  Mighty are we!
The bits and bridles flash in the sunlight,
As all of them ride in pursuit at full gallop:
The horsemen who worship their goddess, Athene,
And Rhea's loved son, earth-circling Poseidon,
  Lord of the sea.

Have they found them yet? Are they fighting?
  My soul is prophetic! I know
The maidens will soon stand before us,
Freed from their hard-hearted kinsman.   1040
Zeus will be with us; some wonder
  To-day he will work on the foe!
O, to soar like a dove to the heavens,
With the speed and strength of a whirlwind,
  To view the battle below!

Zeus, all-ruling, all-seeing
  Lord of Olympus, O hear!
Hear, dread Athene, his daughter!
Make strong the fighters who guard us,
And crown with success their endeavors!   1050
  Phoebus, thou hunter, draw near!
Succor this land and this people,
Thou, and thy sister who follows
  The dappled, fleet-footed deer.

And now, my friend, you will not need to accuse
Your watchman of false prophecy. I see
Your daughters coming, and an escort with them.

OEDIPUS:
  Where? Where? What are you saying?

116

Enter ANTIGONE, ISMENE, THESEUS, *and his* ATTENDANTS

ANTIGONE:

                            Father! Father!
  If only some god would let you see this man,
  This noble man who has brought us back to you!   1060

OEDIPUS:

  Daughter! Are you both there? AN.: Yes. These strong hands
  Have rescued us—Theseus and his kind friends.

OEDIPUS:

  Antigone, here! Here to your father's arms!
  I had given up hope of holding you again.

ANTIGONE:

  Yes, Father, yes. Your wish and mine are one.

OEDIPUS:

  Where are you, then, where are you? AN.: We are coming.

OEDIPUS (*embracing them*):

  My dear, dear children! AN.: A father loves his own.

OEDIPUS:

  Staffs that support my age! AN.: Who suffer with you.

OEDIPUS:

  My dearest daughters! Life would be not all sorrow,
  If I should die with you here in my arms.   1070
  Press closely to me; cling to your father's side.
  Rest there, for you were forced away, forlorn
  And desolate. Tell me what happened, briefly.
  A young girl should not talk at any length.

ANTIGONE:

  I will say little. Here is the man who saved us,
  And he should be the one to tell the story.

OEDIPUS:

  Sir, do not wonder that I give my daughters
  A welcome so prolonged, so deeply felt.
  They were restored when I had lost all hope
  Of seeing them again. You, you alone   1080
  Made this joy possible. You, you alone
  Have rescued them. May all the gods reward you,
  You and your country, even as I would do;
  For only here in Athens have I found
  Truth, piety, and justice. I can give
  Only these words by way of recompense:
  All that I have I have from you alone.
  Stretch forth your hand, O King, that I may touch it,
  And kiss your cheek, if such an act is lawful.
  No! No! What have I said? How could I hope   1090
  To have you touch me—me, a wretched outcast,

Steeped in corruption? Never! Never! I could not!
No one who has not borne this burden with me
Can share it now. But let me thank you, Theseus,
From where I stand; and let me find you still
Kindly and just as I have always found you.

THESEUS:

The joyful greeting that you gave your children
Does not surprise me, for they *should* come first
In your regard. I value fame that follows
Deeds and not words, as I have proved to you,   1100
Because I have in no way fallen short
Of what I promised you. Here are your daughters,
Alive, untouched, in spite of Creon's threats.
As to the fight, why should I boast of it,
When these two girls will tell you how it was won?
But, Oedipus, advise me on a matter
Which I have just been told of, as I came here.
It seems a trifling thing, yet it is strange;
And men, being mortal, should treat nothing lightly.

OEDIPUS:

I have not heard what happened. Let me know.   1110

THESEUS:

A man has rushed up to Poseidon's altar,
Where I was sacrificing when I first
Came hurrying here to help you. There he sits,
A suppliant of the god. He seems to be
Your kinsman, Oedipus, though not a Theban.

OEDIPUS:

Where does he come from? What does he want of me?

THESEUS:

He only asks a few brief words with you.
You have no need, he says, to feel concerned.

OEDIPUS:

Then why does he need the safety of the altar?

THESEUS:

They say he wants only to talk with you,   1120
And then go back unharmed the way he came.

OEDIPUS:

Who can he be who has sought the god's protection?

THESEUS:

Surely you know of someone who might seek
This favor of you, some kinsman of yours from Argos.

OEDIPUS:

No more, no more, my friend! TH.: What is it troubles you?

OEDIPUS:

Do not ask that of me! TH.: Ask what? Come, tell me.

OEDIPUS:

    I know the suppliant now from what you have said.

THESEUS:

    Who is he? How could I object to him?

OEDIPUS:

    He is my hated son. No one on earth
    Could speak to me whom I would loathe so much.   1130

THESEUS:

    He cannot force you to act against your will.
    Can you be hurt by merely listening to him?

OEDIPUS:

    I hate the very sound of my son's voice.
    Do not compel me to yield to you in this.

THESEUS:

    Does not his being a suppliant compel you?
    Consider, sir. You must respect the god.

ANTIGONE:

    Father, I am young, I know, to give advice,
    But listen to me. Let the King satisfy
    His conscience and do honor to the god,
    And let my brother and Ismene's come.   1140
    You need not fear that anything he might say
    To injure you could shake your resolution.
    To hear him speak—what harm could come of that?
    For wickedness is betrayed by what is spoken.
    He is your son. Whatever wrong he did you,
    However impious or infamous,
    You cannot, cannot do him wrong yourself!
    Let him come, Father! Others besides you
    Have evil children and are quick to anger;
    But they can be persuaded, and their friends   1150
    Cast a charm over them that melts their mood.
    Think of the past. Think of your father and mother,
    And what you have endured because of them.
    You know the evil consequence that follows
    From evil anger. How could you forget,
    Blind as you are? Do not refuse us, Father!
    Those who ask justice should not have to beg.
    Men should repay the benefits they receive.

OEDIPUS:

    The benefit you ask of me is bitter,
    Antigone. But be it as you wish.   1160
    Yet if that man must come, take care, my friend,
    To keep this life of mine out of his clutches.

THESEUS:

> I need not listen twice to such a plea.
> I would not boast, and yet you may be certain
> That you are safe while any god saves me.

Exit THESEUS

CHORUS:

> None but a fool would scorn life that was brief.
> None but a fool would cleave to life too long;
>> For when an old man draws his lingering breath
>> Beyond his fitting season, pain and grief,
> The harsh years' harvesting, upon him throng,   1170
>> And joy is but a phantom of the past.
>>> Then soon or late the doom of Hades, death,
> Comes with no dance, no lyre, no marriage song,
>> And all alike delivers at the last.

> Incomparably best is not to be.
> And next to this, once a man sees the day,
>> Is with all speed to hasten whence he came;
>> After youth's trifling joy, he is not free,
> He must endure his lot as best he may:
>> Envy, sedition, murder, hate, and strife,   1180
>>> Until at length old age, unfriended, lame,
> Reviled, and lonely claims him for its prey:
>> The wretched ending of a wretched life.

> Even such is Oedipus, as old as we.
> And as some cape is lashed on every side
>> By wind-swept surges of the winter sea,
> So on his head dashes the deepening tide
>> Of life-long sorrow, so the great winds blow
> From earliest dawn to sunset, from the bright
> And blazing midday to the dead of night: 1190
>> Unceasing bitterness, unceasing woe.

ANTIGONE:

> Look! It is he, I think, the suppliant.
> Father, he is alone and comes in tears.

OEDIPUS:

> Who is he, Daughter? AN.: The man we thought he was
> From the beginning. Here is Polyneices.

POLYNEICES:

> What shall I do? Sisters, what shall I do?
> Weep for myself, or weep for what I see?
> My father—how he has suffered!—old, an exile
> In a strange land with only you. In rags,
> Foul rags that have infected him for years.   1200

Blinded. His tangled hair stirred by the wind.
His scraps of food to stay his pitiful hunger
No better than all the rest. This I have learned
Too late, too late. No man alive has been
So vile as I have in neglecting you.
I will bear witness to my own misdeeds.
Yet Zeus himself, in everything he does,
Has mercy seated by him on his throne.
May she then come and stand beside you also.
There may be remedy for the wrongs I did you.   1210
They can be made no worse. Why are you silent?
Speak to me, Father! Do not turn away!
What! Send me off? Dishonor me? Not a word
To explain your anger? Sisters, he is your father.
Get him to change his mind. Get him to break
His stern, forbidding silence. Do not let him
Dismiss a suppliant in disgrace, unanswered.

ANTIGONE:

Tell him yourself what sad necessity
Has brought you here. Something in your appeal
May kindle happiness within his heart,   1220
Or your own indignation or compassion
May move even those who are voiceless to reply.

POLYNEICES:

Yes, you are right, Antigone, I will speak,
But first I claim protection from the god
Before whose altar I was found. Your King
Promised that I could come to talk with you
And leave unharmed. I beg you Father, Sisters,
Strangers—I beg you all to keep this promise
Inviolate. Now, Father, let me tell you
Why I have come. I am a fugitive   1230
Because I claimed my right, as first-born son,
To assume your kingship. Therefore my young brother
Drove me away. Eteocles was victorious
Neither by argument nor by force of arms,
But by persuading Thebes to take his part.
The Furies brought this curse upon your house.
So I supposed, and so the oracles told me
In Dorian Argos. There it was I swore
A solemn oath with the most famous warriors
Of all the Apian land to join with them   1240
In leading a seven-fold army against Thebes,
And either dying in a righteous cause,
Or driving out that scoundrel from the country.
What brings me here, then? Father, I have come

With heartfelt prayers to you, mine and my allies',
Who now, the leaders of our seven armies,
Circle the Theban plain: Amphiaráus,
Spearman and augurer without an equal;
Týdeus, the son of Oéneus, from Aetolia;
Argive Etéoclus; Hippómedon,   1250
Sent by his father Tálaos; Cápaneus,
Boasting that he will burn Thebes to the ground;
Parthenopáeus of Arcadia,
Named after Atalanta, long a virgin
Until she gave birth to him, her faithful son;
And I, your son, or yours in name at least,
Even if evil destiny begot me.
We are the leaders of the Argive army
That fearlessly is marching against Thebes.
And we implore you, Father, all of us,   1260
For your own sake and for your daughters' sake,
Not to be bitter, not to be angry with me,
Now that I seek revenge against my brother,
A brother who has robbed me and dispossessed me.
For if there is any truth in oracles,
Victory comes to those whom you befriend.
Therefore I beg you, by all our country's gods,
By our hallowed springs, to hear me, to give way.
Like you, I am a beggar and an outcast.
Like you, I win a home by flattering others,   1270
While back in Thebes—how can I bear the thought?—
Eteocles, puffed up with pride, is King
And laughs at both of us. But if you help me,
I will at one stroke bring him down in ruins,
Drive him to exile, establish you again
In your own home, and take my proper place.
Give your assent, and I make good my boast.
I cannot otherwise return alive.

CHORUS:

Speak to him, Oedipus, as you think best,
But for the King's sake, who has sent him here,   1280
Do not dismiss the man without an answer.

OEDIPUS:

Elders, if anyone except the King
Had sent him here for us to talk together,
He would never have heard my voice. But as it is,
He will be given that honor before he goes,
And what he hears will afford him little pleasure.
You utter scoundrel! When you were the King of Thebes,
As your brother is today, you were the one

122

Who forced me into exile, your own father.
You robbed me of my country; you compelled me   1290
To wear the tatters that you weep to see,
Now that you live in wretchedness like mine.
I have long since ceased to weep. I bear this burden
As long as my life lasts, and never, never
Do I forget that you are a murderer.
For it is you who have dragged me down to this:
You who have thrust me from my home; you, you
Who are responsible for my wandering,
My begging strangers for my daily bread.
I might have died for all you did to help me,   1300
Except for these two daughters. They have nursed me,
Preserved me, tended me, shared in my hardships
Like men and not like women. As for you,
You and your brother are no sons of mine.
The god of vengeance sees you, but his gaze
Will grow yet fiercer if in truth those armies
Are marching against Thebes. For you will never
Capture that city. Rather you will die
Bathed in Eteocles' blood, and he in yours.
I cursed you two. I curse you now again.   1310
For you, unlike your sisters, must be taught
To honor parenthood, taught not to scorn
So utterly as you have your sightless father.
Scorn from such sons! My curses have control
Over your suppliance and your talk of thrones,
If truly ancient Justice sits with Zeus
Under the sanction of the eternal laws.
No man on earth could be as vile as you!
I cast you off with loathing, I disown you.
Go! With this final curse called down upon you.   1320
I pray the gods that you may never conquer
Your people or their city, never return
Alive to the vale of Argos. May you kill
The brother who has driven you from your country,
And die yourself, struck down by your brother's hand.
I call on Darkness, the primeval father,
To bring you to the hateful gloom of Hades.
I call on the dread goddesses of this place.
I call on Ares the destroyer, he
Who put this bitter hatred in your hearts.   1330
Now go, since I have spoken to you. Go
Publish these words of mine to all the Thebans,
And tell your trusty allies these are the honors
That Oedipus has bestowed upon his sons.

CHORUS:

> We cannot approve your journeys, Polyneices,
> To Argos or Colonus. Go at once.

POLYNEICES:

> All come to nothing! All our hopes, our efforts!
> When we set out from Argos, what a goal
> We were to reach! This goal! I do not dare
> Speak of it to my friends or turn them back.   1340
> I must go on in silence to my fate.
> Antigone, Ismene, you have heard
> His bitter curses, his unmerciful prayer.
> If he can bring to pass these dreadful things,
> If you return to Thebes, by all the gods!
> Let me not be dishonored, bury me,
> Give me the funeral rites that I should have.
> You have been praised already for what you did
> To help your father, and what you do for me
> Will win you added praise no less deserved.   1350

ANTIGONE:

> Brother, I ask only one thing of you.

POLYNEICES:

> Dearest Antigone, what is it? Tell me.

ANTIGONE:

> Turn back your army to Argos. Now. At once.
> Do not destroy yourself and ruin Thebes.

POLYNEICES:

> Impossible. How could I ever again
> Command that army once I had proved a coward?

ANTIGONE:

> But why should you grow angry ever again?
> What would you gain by laying waste your city?

POLYNEICES:

> My life is shameful. I am an exile, mocked
> By my younger brother—I, the eldest born.   1360

ANTIGONE:

> Do you see you are making your father's words come true?
> He has foretold that you will kill each other.

POLYNEICES:

> Because he wishes it. I cannot yield.

ANTIGONE:

> Brother! Brother! But who will dare to follow
> When he has heard what has been prophesied?

POLYNEICES:

> I will tell no one. A good leader's duty
> Is to reveal what helps and not what hinders.

ANTIGONE:

> Are you determined to do this, Polyneices?

POLYNEICES:

Yes. Do not hold me back. My time has come
To take that dark, ill-fated journey, cursed   1370
By my father and his Furies. As for you two,
May Zeus be gracious to you, if you give me
My rightful honors after I am dead,
Since while I live you can do nothing more.
Now, Sister, let me go. Bid me good-bye.
You will not see me alive again. AN.: No! No!

POLYNEICES:

Do not shed tears for me. AN.: Who would not weep
To see you hurrying open-eyed to death?

POLYNEICES:

If I must die, I must. AN.: Oh Brother, listen!

POLYNEICES:

Only to what is right. AN.: I cannot bear   1380
The thought of losing you. POLY.: Fate will decide
One way or the other. But I pray the gods
You two at least may meet with no misfortune.
No one believes that you deserve to suffer.

Exit POLYNEICES

CHORUS:

Even now we have heard the sightless stranger
  Call down new curses heavy with pain.
Or it may be that fate on its course is keeping,
  For the gods' decrees are not uttered in vain.
They are watched forever by time unsleeping—
  Time, breaking today some fortunes asunder,   1390
And raising others tomorrow on high.

(*a peal of thunder is heard*)

Zeus defend us! That fearful thunder!
  It splits the sky!

OEDIPUS:

Children! Children! Have Theseus brought to me!
Is there a messenger? The King should be here.

ANTIGONE:

Why, Father, why? What do you want of him?

OEDIPUS:

With his swift thunder Zeus has summoned me.
I am to die. Send for the King! Send quickly!

(*a second peal of thunder*)

CHORUS:

> Terror grips me beyond all telling!
>> Again Zeus hurls his thunder! Again! 1400
> Fiercer the bolt falls! Louder it crashes!
>> My hair stirs with horror! Never in vain
> Across the heaven the lightning flashes!
> What black event does its blaze betoken?
>> What woe will follow its wrath let loose?
> My blood runs cold! The sky has spoken!
>> Spare us, O Zeus!

OEDIPUS:

> Children, your father's life draws to a close,
> He faces his inevitable end.

ANTIGONE:

> How have you learned this? Why are you so sure? 1410

OEDIPUS:

> I know beyond all doubt. Lose not a moment.
> Let someone go and bring King Theseus here.

(a third peal of thunder)

CHORUS:

> Once more, once more!
> The world is ringing with that hideous roar!
> Zeus, if thou bringest evil on our land,
>> O stay thy hand!
> Be merciful to us. Free us from our fear.
> Thy doom has come upon this stranger here.
> Let it not now descend upon us all.
>> To thee, Lord Zeus, to thee we call! 1420

OEDIPUS:

> Child, has he come? Will I be still alive,
>> By the time he gets here? Will I have gone mad?

ANTIGONE:

> What comfort, what assurance can he give you?

OEDIPUS:

> When he protected me, I promised him
> Due recompense, and I would keep my word.

CHORUS:

> Theseus, my son!
> If you are honoring the god, have done
> With any sacrifice you might have made,
>> Deep in the glade.
> Come quickly! You, and all who are your own, 1430
> Win the reward of kindness you have shown,
> Share in the blessing Oedipus will bring.
>> Make haste, make haste to us, O King!

Enter THESEUS

THESEUS:

I have heard your summons, Oedipus, and yours,
Men of Colonus. Why are you so anxious?
Is it the thunder or a burst of hail?
For all of us have reason to be fearful
When heaven sends down a storm like this upon us.

OEDIPUS:

Welcome, King Theseus! I have been longing for you.
The gods will bless you for your coming here.   1440

THESEUS:

What is it, son of Laius? What has happened?

OEDIPUS:

I have reached life's utmost verge. Before I die
I wish to keep the promise that I made you.

THESEUS:

How can you be so certain of your fate?

OEDIPUS:

The gods themselves have heralded their tidings.
They have fulfilled what they long since foretold.

THESEUS:

What are the signs that have made their purpose clear?

OEDIPUS:

Long peals of thunder; flash after flash of lightning,
Hurled by the hand of strength invincible.

THESEUS:

I cannot doubt you. I have already heard you   1450
Prophesy truly. Tell me what I must do.

OEDIPUS:

Your city, son of Aegeus, will store up
What I am now to show you as a treasure
Beyond the reach of time. I need no guide,
For I, unaided, will lead you to the place
Where I must die. Never to mortal man
Make known its secret, so that forevermore
It may safeguard you better than a wall
Of native shields, better than alien spears
Of neighboring allies. There, a mystery,   1460
Too sacred to be given utterance,
Will be unfolded only to you King Theseus.
I cannot tell your people or my children,
Dear though they are to me. No, you alone
Must guard this revelation till your life
Draws to a close, and then to your successor,
To him, alone, disclose it. Let him likewise
Instruct his heir, and so through future ages.

Then will this city be secure from Thebes,
The dragon's brood. For states will wantonly   1470
Insult their innocent neighbors since they know
The gods, though sure, are slow to punish men
Who in their frenzy slight religious duty.
May such a fate as that never befall you!
All this you know. I have no need to tell you.
But the gods call. I have felt their urgent summons.
Let us no longer shrink or hesitate.
Follow me, children. Now, in some strange manner,
I am the guide of those who guided me.
Do not so much as lay a finger on me.   1480
I make my own way to that sacred tomb
Where destiny has decreed that I be buried.
Come here! Come here! Hermes and the great goddess
Ruling in Hades lead me on. O light,
Long lost to me, once mine in olden days!
For the last time my living body feels you,
As the dark underworld envelops me.
O friend most dear to me! may all good fortune
Come to your land, your followers, and you!
And that your happiness may evermore   1490
Be at its height, remember me, the dead.

Exeunt OEDIPUS, THESEUS, ANTIGONE, ISMENE

CHORUS:

If any prayer may be addressed to thee,
   Hear us, Persephone,
Dread goddess hidden from our mortal sight!
Lord Hades, hear, god of the land of night!
   Grant that our friend may go,
Not sorrowful, not suffering from his doom,
   Down to the dead below,
Down to the Stygian fields' enshrouding gloom.
   From his unmerited misery   1500
May the gods now in justice set him free.

Avenging Furies in your dark domain,
   Have pity on his pain!
Unconquered Cerberus, who dost lie in wait
Guarding that wide and ever-welcoming gate,
   Snarling within thy lair,
Thou mighty monster, be thou good to us!
   O Death, hear thou our prayer,
Thou terrible son of Earth and Tartarus!
   Make clear his pathway to the deep   1510
O thou, the giver of eternal sleep.

Enter MESSENGER

MESSSENGER:

My friends, this is the substance of my message:
Oedipus is no more. But the whole story
Of all that has taken place cannot be brief.

CHORUS:

He is no longer suffering? He is dead?

MESSSENGER:

You may be certain his last day has come.

CHORUS:

What did the gods decree? A painless doom?

MESSSENGER:

Wonderful things have happened. You all know,
Since you were here yourselves, how Oedipus left you
With no one guiding him, for he himself   1520
Showed us the way. Now when he reached the chasm
Where the bronze steps lead down precipitously,
He paused by one of many branching paths
By the rock-basin, the memorial
Of the unbroken pact Peirithous
Made with King Theseus. There he stood midway
Between this basin, the Thorician stone,
The hollow pear-tree, and the marble tomb.
Then he sat down, loosened his sordid garments,
And summoning his daughters, bade them bring him   1530
Water from some pure spring, that he might wash
And pour out a drink-offering to the dead.
So from Demeter's hillside, close at hand,
Quickly they brought all that their father asked for,
Washed him, and clothed him as is customary,
Neglecting nothing that could satisfy him.
Then the god thundered, Zeus of the world of darkness.
The two girls, shuddering, fell at their father's knees,
Burst into tears, and beat their breasts, lamenting
Loudly and long. At their sharp, sudden cry   1540
He folded them in his arms. 'Children,' he said,
'You have no father now. My life is over,
And your sad task of tending me is done,
A heavy burden, I know, for you to bear.
Yet there is one word—love—that makes the hardships
That you have suffered seem of no importance.
No one has given you love as great as mine.
Now you must live without me through the years
That are before you.' So in the utmost grief
They all embraced. At last their tears ceased flowing,   1550
Their loud sobs died away, and there was silence.

Then suddenly a terrifying voice,
A god's voice echoing and re-echoing,
Standing their hair on end, rang out in summons:
'Oedipus, Oedipus, why do we delay?
Already you have lingered here too long.'
Knowing a god had called him, Oedipus
Asked Theseus to draw near, and at his coming
Said to him, 'Dearest friend, here are my daughters.
Give them your hand—and children, give him yours—   1560
Promise me always to be kind to them,
Always to do what you think best for them.'
Checking his grief, high-minded as he is,
King Theseus made this promise. Thereupon,
Oedipus, groping blindly for his daughters,
Said to them, 'Children, courage! You must go.
Do not ask to see or hear forbidden things.
Leave this place quickly, but let the King remain,
Whose right it is to witness what will happen.'
Hearing him speak these words, we turned away   1570
With the two women, weeping bitterly.
And then, a little later, we looked back.
There was no sign of Oedipus to be seen,
And Theseus stood with his hand before his face,
Shielding his eyes, like one who beheld some sight
So awful as to be unendurable.
Then he began to pray, bowing in worship
Of earth and of the heavens. In what manner
Oedipus met his doom no mortal knows
Other than Theseus. In that final moment,   1580
No flash of lightning made an end of him,
Nor sudden tempest springing from the sea.
Either some messenger of the gods arrived,
Or the foundations of the earth split open
To take him without pain, indulgently.
His going was not marked by lamentation,
Sickness, or suffering. No one has ever met
An end so marvelous. If anyone here
Feels that such things are unbelievable,
I will not try to persuade him of their truth.   1590

CHORUS:

Where are the women now? Where are their friends?

MESSSENGER:

They are not far away. The sounds of mourning,
Broken and indistinct, tell they are coming.

Enter ANTIGONE *and* ISMENE

ANTIGONE:

 Gone! Gone! He is gone! Most miserable are we,
  Wailing with grief's full flood
 The fatal heritage of our father's blood.
  For his sake, in the past,
 Of his unending pain we endured our share.
  And now, now at the last,
 Beyond belief is the sight we have had to see,   1600
  Beyond belief the loss we have had to bear.

CHORUS: What loss, my child? AN.: That we can never know.

CHORUS: Then he is gone? AN.: As you would want him to go.
 For not in battle, not in the salt sea wave,
  Did he cease to be;
 But strangely and swiftly he was snatched away
  To those dim fields far from the light of day.
 We are in darkness, the darkness of the grave!
  How shall we live, in our extremity
 Evermore wandering over land and sea?   1610

ISMENE: I do not know. Would that my life might end,
 End in the depths of Hades, with my father!
  The life that lies ahead cannot be borne.

CHORUS: Kindest and best of daughters, you have been blameless.
  Do not too long, too passionately mourn.
 Men must accept what fate the gods may send.

ANTIGONE: Ah! Now at length I have come to find it true:
  We long to have again
 The vanished past, in spite of all its pain.
  To hold him in my embrace   1620
 Was to find happiness at the heart of woe.
  Though we see no more your face,
 Still, Father, still our love goes out to you,
  Even to the darkness of the world below.

CHORUS: The world below? AN.: At long last he is there.

CHORUS: He has found rest? AN.: Rest in the shadowed air
 That he has yearned for, in the nether deep,
  Where the dead abide.
 And I abide here in my bitter grief!
  When from this anguish will I find relief?   1630
 O Father! Father! when will I cease to weep?
  You had your wish: in a strange land you died.
 But I was not there! Not there! Not at your side!

ISMENE: What new misfortunes are before us still,
 Now we are left alone, homeless, and orphaned?
  Sister, what has the future now in store?

CHORUS: Painlessly, blessedly, his life has ended.
        Children, give way to this lament no more.
    Never is man beyond the reach of ill.

ANTIGONE: Come back, come back, Ismene! Come with me!   1640
ISMENE: What will you do? AN.: A fever consumes me. IS.: Sister!
ANTIGONE: There is one dark resting-place that I must see.
ISMENE: Antigone! Whose? AN.: You know it is our father's.
ISMENE: We cannot. You heard the command our father gave.
ANTIGONE: Why are you disapproving? Why do you speak so?
ISMENE: We were to leave— AN.: What more have you to say?
ISMENE: He was to die alone, without a grave.
ANTIGONE: Then take me to the spot and let me perish!
ISMENE: How can I live? Where can I make my way,
        Friendless and helpless?   1650

CHORUS: Do not grieve so, my child. You need not fear.
ISMENE: But where shall I fly? CH.: You have a refuge. IS.: Refuge?
CHORUS: Here in our midst. No harm can touch you here.
ISMENE: I am sure of that. CH.: Then tell me why you are troubled.
ISMENE: I long to go home, to go home! But I know not how.
CHORUS: Do not go home. Stay with us here in safety.
ISMENE: Harsh, harsh is our fate. CH.: Blow upon grievous blow.
ISMENE: Hopeless before, and worse than hopeless now.
CHORUS: Truly a sea of sorrow broke upon you.
ISMENE: What can we do? Zeus! Zeus! Where can we go?   1660
        What hope is left us?

Enter THESEUS

THESEUS:
    My daughters, weep no more. The gods of Hades
    Have shown their great beneficence to us all,
    The living and the dead. Further lament
    Would bring their anger down upon our heads.
ANTIGONE:
    Hear, son of Aegeus! Hear our supplication!
THESEUS:
    What would you ask of me, Antigone?
ANTIGONE:
    That we ourselves might see our father's grave.
THESEUS:
    I cannot let you, child. It is forbidden.
ANTIGONE:
    How can that be, O King, O Lord of Athens?   1670

THESEUS:

>Daughters, your father laid this charge upon me:
>No one was to draw near his resting place,
>No utterance was to break the holy silence.
>If I performed this duty faithfully,
>I would preserve my country from all harm.
>These things I promised him, and the great gods
>Before whom oaths are sacred heard me swear.

ANTIGONE:

>I say no more. What was our father's pleasure
>Must satisfy us. Send us back to Thebes,
>Our ancient land, for there we yet may save   1680
>Our brothers from the death that threatens them.

THESEUS:

>Yes, you shall go. I will not spare myself
>In giving you whatever help I can,
>For your sakes and for his whom death has taken.

CHORUS:

>Come, daughters. Cease to grieve, cease to lament.
>No longer mourn for him, no longer wail.
>These things have been established. Be content.
>For what the gods establish cannot fail.

26 The Greeks believed that the dead refused to associate with the spirits of those who had not been buried.

49 According to the *Iliad* (23. 679ff) Oedipus met a violent death at Thebes. In his later play, *Oedipus at Colonus*, Sophocles has Oedipus meet a mysterious but sacred end, being snatched away in some unknown fashion by the gods.

101 The river Dircé was to the west of Thebes, the river Ismenus to the east.

110 The dragon is the Theban army. The Thebans were descendants of men sprung from the dragon's teeth sown by Cadmus.

116–18 The reference is to the giant Capaneus, who boasted that he would burn Thebes to the ground. As he scaled the walls, Zeus killed him with a bolt of lightning.

118 Ares was the god of war.

126 Niké was the goddess of victory.

129 Dancing was a conspicuous feature of the worship of Bacchus.

147 Creon was a first cousin of Laius. He had been Regent and was now King in his own right.

287–9 Creon's irony is grim. The guard will have learned his lesson only after he is dead.

389 It is not clear why Antigone returned to the body. She had already sprinkled it with dust. Perhaps the rite was not complete unless the libation was poured while the body was still covered.

416 The reference is to the gods of the underworld.

431 Oedipus's quick temper was a contributing factor in his downfall.

526 Creon is unjust to Haemon in thinking that he could have chosen what Creon has just called 'an evil bride.'

543 The Greek has 'the house of Labdacus.' See Introduction.

562–3 The image is presumably that of walking over ashes under which fire still smoulders.

567 He had one other son, Mendeceus or Megareus. See line 1231.

756 Hades, the brother of Zeus, was the King of the underworld.

135

757   Acheron was the River of Sorrow, one of the four rivers of the underworld.

767   Niobe was the wife of Amphíon, regent of Thebes after the death of King Pentheus. During the ceremonies in honor of the goddess Leto and her children Apollo and Artemis, Niobe boasted of herself and her fourteen children in comparison to the goddess with her two. In revenge Leto had all of Niobe's children killed and Niobe herself transformed into a stone from which a stream of water continually flowed.

774   Antigone has compared herself to Niobe—she feels as Niobe did when she was turning into stone. The chorus try to console her by reminding her that it is splendid for a mortal to become comparable to a goddess. Antigone, however, feels that they are mocking her because she had hoped to receive pity for her present condition and not praise for posthumous fame.

801   Polyneices married Argeia, daughter of the King of Argos, to secure his help in the war against Thebes. Hence Polyneices was the ultimate cause of Antigone's death.

824   Persephone was the Queen of the underworld.

829   Eteocles is the brother referred to here.

868   Various members of the royal house of Thebes were the children of gods or married gods.

873   She ignores Ismene, perhaps because she feels that, at least in spirit, she is the last of her race.

877–908   The chorus cites three other occasions on which royal personages were cruelly imprisoned as illustrations of the general truth that no mortal can resist fate. Two of the victims were innocent, one was guilty. Hence the chorus implies nothing concerning Antigone's guilt.

877   Danaë was imprisoned by her father Acrisius, the King of Argos, because an oracle told him that her son would kill him. Zeus, however, visited her in the guise of a shower of gold. She bore Perseus, who later accidentally killed Acrisius.

885–92   Lycurgus, King of Edonia in Thrace, for opposing the rites of Dionysus (the maenads were his female votaries) was driven mad by the gods. His violence was so great that an oracle commanded his subjects to imprison him in a cave. He was later killed by wild beasts.

893–908   Cleopatra, daughter of Boreas, god of the north wind, was divorced and imprisoned by King Phineus. He then married again, and his new wife blinded and imprisoned Cleopatra's two sons.

968–72   In his anger Creon has imagined the most terrible of pollutions, and then excuses his impiety by citing a general religious maxim.

1009   The cities referred to are the ones which had sent armies against Thebes.

1045–8 Bacchus or Dionysus, the god of wine, was the son of Semele and Zeus. She insisted that Zeus visit her in his own likeness. Accordingly he came armed with thunderbolts and in a blaze of lightning which destroyed her, although her unborn son was saved.

1050   Icaria was a district of Attica, associated with Dionysus. It is possible that the text should read 'Italian.'

1052   Eleusis is on the coast of Attica. The Eleusinian Festivals and Mysteries were in honor of Persephone (see line 824) and her mother Demeter, or Ceres, goddess of the earth, and in particular of agriculture.

1057   Cadmus, the founder of Thebes, slew a dragon and sowed its teeth which sprang up as armed men, the ancestors of the Thebans.

1060   Parnassus was a mountain sacred to Apollo and the Muses.

1063   The 'stream' was a spring on Parnassus sacred to Apollo and the Muses. Those who drank from it or bathed in it received poetic inspiration.

1065   Nysa was on the island of Euboea, off the coast of Attica.

1073   Semele. See line 1045.

1075   Separating Euboea from the mainland.

1084   Amphion. See line 767. His skill in music was so great that the walls of Thebes rose to the sound of his lyre.

1127ff It is hard to see why Creon, who was hurrying to save Antigone, stopped first to bury Polyneices. Jebb, the chief editor of Sophocles, suggests that Sophocles was influenced by considerations of rhetoric. If the messenger had first described the scene at the tomb and then the burial of Polyneices, his speech would have been anticlimactic.

1169   In lines 1152–4 Haemon was embracing her yet hanging body. Here it is stretched on the ground.

1231–2 See line 567. Megareus allowed himself to be killed early in the attack in order to fulfill an oracle and save Thebes. It is not clear why Eurydice accuses Creon of being responsible for his death.

8   This is the frankness of an epic hero. It is magnanimity in Aristotle's sense, rather than pride in the modern sense.

19   Thebes was divided into an eastern and a western section by the river Strophia. There was a market place in each section.

20   Each market place would have its shrine.

20–21   The Greek has 'the oracular ashes of Ismenus.' The reference was to the temple of Apollo beside the river Ismenus, where divination by burnt offerings was practiced.

36–7   The Greek has 'the tribute we paid to the harsh songstress.' The Sphinx, a winged monster with a lion's body and a woman's head and breasts, compelled all passers-by to answer her riddle and killed all who failed to answer it correctly. Sophocles calls her a songstress because a riddle such as hers was associated in folklore with the incantations of sorcery and witchcraft. When Oedipus gave the correct answer, the Sphinx committed suicide. The riddle was this: 'What animal is it that goes in the morning on four feet, at noon on two, and in the evening on three?' The answer is man, who crawls in infancy, walks erect in manhood, and uses a staff in old age. The symbolism of the myth is clear: to solve the riddle Oedipus had to understand the essential nature of man. Such understanding is possesssed only by a man of wisdom.

72   This was the temple of Apollo at Delphi. Pytho was the old name for the district. The name of the priestess was the Pythia.

113ff   It is highly improbable that Oedipus has never learned of the facts of King Laius's death.

145   Cadmus was the founder of Thebes.

152   The Chorus consists of the elders of Thebes, men of noble birth.

152   The Chorus speaks euphemistically of the oracle, which they have not yet heard.

161   The oracle is the response to the Theban's inquiry; hence, the child or issue of their hope.

164   The statue of Artemis was in the market place.

179   The reference here is to the god of the next world, which was traditionally in the west.

188   Ares was the god of war, here identified with the plague.

249–50   There is an ironic ambiguity in the original. Laius and Oedipus *did* have children in common: Oedipus himself and Oedipus's children. The Greek means both 'if he (Laius) had not been ill-fated in his son (in having no son)' or 'If his son (Oedipus) had not been ill-fated.' The translation has tried to reproduce this effect. Certainly Oedipus is not a blessing either to himself or to Laius.

254   The Greek lists the ancestors: (Laius) the son of Labdacus, son of Polydorus, son of Cadmus, son of Agenor (King of Phoenicia).

278   This report is closer to the truth than the earlier one that the killers were robbers (124), but Oedipus does not distinguish between them.

371   The Sphinx was sent to afflict the city by Hera, who hated Thebes because it was the city of her rival Semele, mother of Dionysus.

461   The temple of Delphi was regarded as the center of the earth. In it a stone marked the spot at which the eagles flying from the east and the west had met.

469–71   The Greek has: 'I have never heard of any quarrel between the house of Labdacus or the son of Polybus.' The Greek audience was familiar with the actual lineage of Oedipus and with the fact that he was thought to be the son of Polybus, King of Corinth. This is the first reference in the play to Polybus, who is unknown to a modern audience. The point is too important dramatically to be left obscure.

592   Two or three lines are here omitted. The original text is corrupt and probably defective.

682   Sophocles ignores the fact that Jocasta, since her marriage to Oedipus, must have seen his scarred feet. Nor does Oedipus refer to them until much later in the play.

720   This is inconsistent with the account in 119–132. The Sphinx prevented a thorough investigation of the murder, and Oedipus did not arrive until considerably later.

721   The Greek has 'with his hand laid on mine.' This act, like clasping the knees, marks a formal petition.

769   The driver was probably on foot, leading the horses up hill.

865   The Jebb translation has: 'a branch wreathed with festoons of wool.'

989   Oedipus means swollen foot.

1175.   The Ister was the lower Danube. The Phasis was a river of Colchis, a country between the Black Sea and the Caspian Sea. It was famous in connection with the expedition of the Argonauts.

1222–3   Oedipus is referring to his children.

1224   Here he refers to his parents, whose identity he had long sought and whom he had failed to recognize.

1245   The kommos, or lyric passage, begins here, although the system of strict strophe and antistrophe does not begin until 1263.

1423–6   Athenian women could appear in public only on special occasions. Ismene and Antigone, polluted by the family curse, would be exposed to comment or insult.

14–15   Antigone is referring to the city walls, and probably also to the Acropolis, of Athens, a little more than a mile away.

41   The Eumenides was a euphemistic title for the Erinyes, or Furies, the daughters of Earth and Hades. (Other genealogies are given elsewhere.) Fearful winged maidens with serpents twined in their hair and with blood dripping from their eyes, they punished men both in this world and after death.

42   There were other daughters of Darkness, for example, the Moirai, or Fates.

58   Poseidon was the god of the sea, son of Cronos and brother of Zeus and Hades. See 672 note, 683 note.

59   Prometheus was not strictly a Titan, but the son of the Titan Iapetus. The Titans were sons of Uranus (Heaven) and Ge (Earth). They overthrew their father and made their youngest brother, Cronos, king. They were in turn overthrown by the son of Cronos, Zeus. Prometheus brought the gift of fire to men by stealing it from the gods. For this Zeus chained him to a rock on Mount Caucasus, where an eagle perpetually devoured his liver. He was eventually freed by Heracles (Hercules). He is called a god because the Titans were divinities and because he was later given immortality by the Centaur Chiron.

59–61   The 'spot' was a steep cleft or a cavern in the rock regarded as the entrance to Hades, at the mouth of which brazen steps had been made. In calling it the mainstay of Athens, Sophocles joins the idea of a literal physical basis with that of a religious safeguard.

63   Colonus, the ordinary word for 'hill,' is here traced back to a mythical individual who gave his name to the spot. He is called a horseman to justify the epithet of 'of horses' given to the place Colonus. The Greek text here reads 'that horseman Colonus,' and there may have been a statue of him on the stage to which the Countryman pointed.

72   Theseus was the great hero of the Athenians and one of their early semi-mythical kings. For his exploits see 535 note

88   Oedipus is calling the Eumenides. See 41 note.

91–4   The prophecy was made to Oedipus at Delphi when he went there as a youth to ask about his parentage.

118   For Athens as the city of Pallas Athene see 672 note.

135   The usual invocation of a deity was, of course, audible, partly from a feeling that one ought not to make any prayer which should not be heard.

140

173 Three lines of the original are here lost.

250 In Oedipus's fight with his father, Laius struck the first blow.

254 Oedipus's father and mother had deliberately tried to kill him through exposure to the elements.

257-8 The men of Colonus are not paying proper respect to the gods because they wish to violate their pledge to the gods' suppliant.

313 Oedipus had two sons: Polyneices, the elder, and Eteocles, the younger.

346 Creon was the brother of Jocasta, Oedipus's mother and wife.

355 Polyneices married the daughter of Adrastus, King of Argos.

395-6 His sons have put their personal ambition ahead of their concern for Oedipus or for Thebes, whose welfare depends on his presence. They could at least have tried to get the Thebans to recall Oedipus to the city, where he could have lived the remainder of his life, even though he could not actually have been buried on Theban soil. Oedipus accuses them of lack of piety and lack of patriotism.

433 Apollo has fulfilled the oracles by bringing him to the grove of the Eumenides.

459 Only pure water is poured from the first two bowls.

513 Oedipus is referring to the gift of Jocasta as his wife because of his solving the riddle of the Sphinx.

535-7 Theseus was born in Troezen, a city in Argos. The most famous of his numerous exploits was the slaying of the Minotaur in the labyrinth of Crete. For his descent to the underworld see 1525 note.

560 Theseus thinks that Oedipus's sons would object to his retaining possession of Oedipus's body.

644 'White' refers either to the light-colored soil, or to the buildings of the hillside town.

649 The Chorus refers to the grove of the Eumenides or the Academy, a grove near Athens sacred to the hero Academus.

649-50 The ivy and the vine were sacred to Dionysus; hence the whole wood is called his.

651 Dionysus was the god of wine. See Antigone, 1045-8 note.

658 The immortals were the two goddesses Demeter, sister of Zeus and goddess of agriculture, and Persephone, her daughter abducted by Hades and made his queen. The narcissus was the flower Persephone was in the act of picking when she was seized. Dionysus is associated with these goddesses in the Eleusinian mysteries.

669   Aphrodite was the goddess of love and beauty. The golden reins were used in driving her chariot drawn by sparrows, swans, or doves.

672   This was the olive tree that sprang from the earth at the command of Athene when she and Poseidon were having a contest for the possession of Athens (Poseidon created a horse), the city going to the one who produced the more useful gift to man.

674   The sacred olives were spared when the Spartans invaded Attica.

677   The Chorus is speaking not of one tree, but the genus, growing throughout Greece.

683   Poseidon created a horse in his contest with Athene (see 672). He taught men to ride, and also, having created the oar, taught men to row.

709   The Thebans were descended from Cadmus.

913   The Hill of Ares was the meeting place of the Areopagus, the criminal court of Athens.

953   Oedipus married as a result of his saving Thebes. See 513 note.

1000–1   This was the conventional explanation of disaster. Sophocles' audience would merely have thought that Theseus was taking sensible precautions.

1018   The enemy is on the shore of the Bay of Eleusis, about six miles from Colonus. There was a temple of Apollo in the pass leading to this spot.

1019–22   The reference is to Eleusis itself, about five miles further from Colonus. The Eleusinian mysteries honored Dionysus as well as Demeter and Persephone.

1023   Theseus is here thought of as personally rescuing the sisters, and later himself speaks of having done so (1104–5). This is inconsistent with his speech to Creon, where their rescue is left to the guards Theseus has sent in pursuit (991–3).

1026   The location of Mount Oea is uncertain. It probably marks an inland route of escape, as opposed to that along the shore mentioned in the preceding strophe.

1053   Phoebus Apollo's twin sister was Artemis, the virgin goddess of the moon and the hunt.

1108–9   Since man cannot read the future, he cannot be sure that an incident, apparently trivial, may not prove important.

1115   Probably his clothes showed that he was not a Theban.

1127   Theseus has said the stranger is from Argos (1124), and Oedipus remembers that Ismene has said that Polyneices had gone there (351–4).

1202 The 'scraps of food' were carried in a beggar's wallet.

1238 The land of the Dorians was the Peloponnesus.

1240 The 'Apian land' was the Peloponnesus. The name is derived from Apis, a mythical king who purged the land of monsters.

1241ff The story of this war has been treated by many Greek writers: Aeschylus, *Seven against Thebes;* Euripides, *Phoenissae, Suppliants,* etc. The expedition failed, and all of these leaders were killed. The two brothers, Eteocles and Polyneices, killed each other. The opening chorus of Sophocles' *Antigone* celebrates the Theban victory.

1247 Amphiaráus foresaw the outcome but was persuaded to go by his wife, who had been bribed by Polyneices.

1251–2 This boasting led to his death. As he was scaling the wall of Thebes, Zeus killed him with a bolt of lightning. See the opening chorus of *Antigone.*

1254 She finally married Milanion, the man who defeated her in a footrace by diverting her attention with three golden apples. Parthenopaéus is named after her because in Greek 'parthenes' means a virgin.

1310 See 398-403.

1313 By Athenian law sons were disfranchised for grave neglect of filial duty, such as failure to support a parent in sickness or old age.

1315 Polyneices, as a suppliant at Poseidon's altar, had begged his father to remember that mercy was enthroned beside Zeus, and as the elder son, had claimed the throne of Thebes.

1346–7 The play of *Antigone* is concerned with her carrying out of these rites.

1355–6 By returning to Argos and starting again, Polyneices might, technically, avoid Oedipus's curse.

1388 Oedipus's recent curse of Polyneices may be new or merely the continued working of the old curse upon his house.

1417–9 Since Oedipus was under a curse and hence polluted, even casual association with him was dangerous.

1443 Oedipus is referring to the promise that he would act as guardian of the country in which he was buried. See 548ff.

1451 Oedipus had predicted trouble between Athens and Thebes (588–592), and Creon's subsequent acts fulfilled the prophecy. At his final exit Creon hinted at future war: 1007-8.

1455–6 This passage identifies the spot where Oedipus will disappear as the spot where he will be buried. This is inconsistent with what is said elsewhere. The place where he disappeared is known, but the secret

143

of his grave is given only to Theseus in a sort of mystic vision (1574–6). Later (1669–77) Theseus shows that he has this knowledge but may not reveal it.

1470 When Cadmus was founding Thebes, he needed water from a well guarded by a dragon, the offspring of Ares. He killed the dragon and sowed its teeth in the ground, on the advice of Athene. Armed men sprang up, who killed each other with the exception of five. These became the ancestors of the Thebans.

1472–3 Oedipus is probably thinking of his sons, who have so far gone unpunished.

1483 Among his many functions, Hermes conducted the shades to the underworld. The goddess was Persephone, daughter of Zeus and Demeter and wife of Hades (see below).

1495 Hades (Aides, or Pluto) was the son of Cronos and Rhea and hence the brother of Zeus and Poseidon. He was the King of the underworld.

1502 The Greek has 'goddesses of the underworld.' They can hardly be Demeter and Persephone, who would not be associated, as here, with Cerberus (see below). For Furies see 41 note.

1504 Cerberus was the fifty-headed dog guarding the entrance to Hades. He was later represented as having three heads and a serpent's tail.

1508 Death, Thanatos, is not elsewhere given this parentage. He is generally spoken of as a son of Night, and as the brother of sleep.

1523 The branching paths are perhaps a deliberate reminder of the fork in the road at which he met and killed his father.

1525 Pirithous was King of the Lapithae in Thessaly. Theseus was present at his wedding and helped him in his fight with the Centaurs, who abducted the bride. After the death of his wife, Pirithous determined to carry off and marry Persephone. Theseus went down to the underworld with him, where both were seized by Pluto and fastened to a rock. Theseus was later rescued by Heracles. In one version of the legend Pirithous was also rescued.

1527 The rock of Thoricos, the pear-tree, and the marble tomb are sacred objects whose significance was unknown, even to early commentators. The passage is of dramatic importance in showing that Oedipus was guided to a spot the peculiar sanctity of which he could not have known.

1535 The dead were dressed for burial in white. Sophocles leaves us to imagine where the clothes were found.

1651ff In this antistrophe, Ismene's speeches are usually given to Antigone. The thought, however, is more appropriate for Ismene. Antigone is obsessed with the idea of visiting her father's grave. It is her first plea to Theseus when he enters.

1676–7 These gods were: the deity that had summoned Oedipus, and Horkos, the god who witnessed an oath and punished perjury.